Why Marriage?

Why marriage?

by EDWARD E. FORD

with Robert L. Zorn, Ph.D.

Foreword by William Glasser, M.D.

ARGUS COMMUNICATIONS

Niles, Illinois

First Edition

Printed in U.S.A.

International Standard Book Number
0-913592-25-0

Library of Congress Catalog Card Number
73-93668

Published by Argus Communications
Niles, Illinois 60648

TO HESTER

and to our three daughters
Dorothy, Terry, and Mary Ellen
and five sons
John, Nelson, Joseph, Thomas, and Luke

Contents

Foreword

Although many people seem to be questioning marriage and trying alternate styles of conjugal living, more people than ever are getting married. While they are marrying a little later, having fewer children, and are accepting more the wife's role as a wage earner, once married they want to stay married. Divorce, while frequent, is never easy. Most divorced people would readily admit that they tried hard to save their marriage and many who also marry for the second time recognize that what they tried in their first marriage was worthwhile but too late. They were just too far apart. In their second marriage they try sooner, often before problems arise, and they remark how much better their second marriage is. If I ask, "Is the second marriage better at the beginning than the first?" they pause and say, "No, but we let the first one fall apart. We just didn't realize that love and new sex are not enough to keep two people together." People do learn from painful experience, but for many the lesson is too late. It is to this concern, that people learn to trust each other and work continuously to make their marriage a success, that this book is dedicated.

People will find the ideas of *Why Marriage?* work if they are used. They are based upon the sound concepts of involvement and problem solving, the idea that people can direct their lives together and need not drift apart because they do not know what to do. I especially urge young people to read this book before they get married and I hope that schools, counselors, ministers, and parents not only make it available, but then take the time and discuss its contents so that young people can be better prepared for marriage. If marriage as an institution fails, our society will be cast adrift. *Why Marriage?* will help prevent this from happening.

William Glasser, M.D.

Preface

and acknowledgements

Down through the ages when men of great creativity have written new and exciting ideas, many who have known them and who have liked what these men had to say then attempted to popularize what was said. This is what I have attempted to do with the creative thoughts of Dr. William Glasser, author of *Reality Therapy*, *Schools Without Failure* and *The Identity Society*.

The impact of Dr. Glasser's ideas has yet to be fully realized, but the simplicity and profoundness of his words are having wide acceptance. Those who hear and read what he has to say have said these ideas "make sense" and "they work." I see this book as one of many which will attempt to popularize Reality Therapy for the general public.

I suppose this book got its start while I was teaching at Ursuline High School in Youngstown in the 1960s. The young girls I taught kept asking me about love and marriage and what made relationships work and endure. My attempt to answer their questions led me inevitably to this book and thus my acknowledgement to them as both a source who gave me confidence in myself and an incentive to go on. Their faith in me as teacher and counselor is something I shall never forget.

A good friend, Dr. Arthur LeBlanc, a Los Angeles clinical psychologist whose own keen insights and understandings of Reality Therapy have been most helpful, once said that the future books of psychology will be "handbooks for daily living." I see this work as such a book.

I wish to express my appreciation to Joy Gaetano, who patiently typed and retyped the manuscript during the many rewritings.

Also, my thanks to Joan Zorn and her daughters, Debbie and Patty, for their patience and kindness over the past year while Bob and I were writing this book.

And finally to Bob Zorn, whose writing along with his own keen insights made this book possible. Without him, this book would have never become a reality.

Youngstown, Ohio
November 18, 1973

Edward E. Ford

Introduction

What is reality therapy?

Reality Therapy recognizes that the basic need of mankind is to attain a *success identity*. The pathway to a success identity or self-image is through developing an ability to make and maintain genuine human relationships . . . and through seeing oneself as a worthwhile person, both in one's own eyes and in the eyes of others, in terms of what one actually does.

It assumes we all have the same needs but we vary in our ability to fulfill them . . . that to be worthwhile we must maintain a satisfactory standard of behavior . . . that responsible individuals fulfill their needs in a way that does not infringe on the rights of others nor deprive others of the ability to fulfill their needs.

Reality Therapy is a method of working with people. It states that a person is responsible for his own behavior–not society, not the environment, not heredity, not the past, but each person now. Reality Therapy urges individuals to gain the strength to change through involvement with others. It is through this human relationship, this honest interest in others, that people who believe they are doomed to failure can regain their self-respect and self-confidence.

Reality Therapy states that people who fail in life do so because they have made poor choices of behavior due to an inability to become involved in authentic human relationships. To make better choices these "failures" must first learn to become honestly involved with others.

They must also be taught both to evaluate what they are doing and how to plan a better way of living their life. Although they feel bad, it is only through changing their behavior that they will eventually begin to feel better.

Reality Therapy is not a textbook. It is life. It is action. It is hard work. It is the *way* you live . . . with yourself and with others.

Chapter one

This book

Progress or perish . . . Don't be left behind . . . The world is in a hurry . . . Pressures. We are all being pressured to live faster, to step up the pace in our lives. This fact is self-evident; the reason for it is not. Our goals, once set by the economic and religious underpinnings of society, are no longer clear. Life styles have changed in the past decade. A generation ago we wouldn't have known what the words "life style" meant.

We are living in a world of throw-away products—and some say also a world of throw-away friends because of our mobility. Transfers, advancement, changing jobs, these once-earthshaking decisions have become routine. And now, throw-away marriages seem to be part of the pattern.

Newer, more challenging problems are facing us in the 1970s. Women are redefining their role and most men merely witness with incredulity this overdue assertion of equality. It should come as no surprise, then, that at a time when our society is in a condition of radical transition, even good marriages are experiencing the stress of change.

In the "good old days" couples whose marriages survived the economic ordeal of making ends meet were considered to have had a successful marriage. Today an additional criterion has been added. Young couples are in search of something beyond mere economic stability. They are looking for a relationship with each other that will grow and develop. They also are looking for growth as individuals.

Not long ago a woman might ask, "Do you still love me?" and her husband would reply, "Don't I kill myself supporting this family?" And his wife would be satisfied. Things are changing. Today such a question might be put this way: "Do you really love me? Or am I just a live-in maid with master bedroom privileges?" And many a husband will be hard pressed to provide an easy answer.

Divorce was taboo a generation ago. Now it is not uncommon to hear, "Most of my friends have either been divorced or are thinking about it." Once a last resort, divorce is often now the second paragraph on the agenda of a squabbling couple, preceded only by a list of grievances. Once a man might spend hours away from home for such unexplained but obvious reasons as business or golf. Today his wife will ask, "What about me? What about your children?"

Look at the change in the role of a mother. Not long ago, the vast majority of unwed mothers gave up their babies. Now there is less and less of a stigma attached to being a single parent. Young girls don't worry as much anymore about unwanted pregnancies. There is more concern about syphilis or gonorrhea, but these are manageable. On Saturday nights in the 1940s and the 1950s, adventuring couples necked and petted in cars parked on a lover's lane. Now many

find their excitement in a motel room, an apartment or group sexual encounter. Not everyone is this "emancipated," but times have changed!

The cinema of the Pat Boone era—with the clean-cut wholesomeness approach—has given way to movies with anything from nudity to explicit sex. We are finding it harder and harder to find a family-oriented movie.

Even the stereotype of the dirty old man seducing a young female has a new variation. We are now introduced to the older woman and her young male companion. To the problem of female frigidity we have added the problem of male impotency. To the perennial female pin-ups we have added the center-fold of such male sex images as Burt Reynolds and George Maharis.

Ms. and *Playgirl* attest to the rapidly changing times. When we consider readers' mores today as compared with a generation ago, the contrast is remarkable. What happened to such old-time favorites as *Colliers* and the *Saturday Evening Post*? Toffler's book *Future Shock* is no longer shocking. From rural to urban. From single dwellings to highrises. From scarcity to plenty. From radio to TV. From DC-3 to spaceships. From gunpowder to A-bomb. From oppression to liberation. From big business to Ralph Nader. From survival and security to identity and self-image.

But what has really changed? How has this change in American society affected married life? I want to discuss these changing relationships and how we might learn to cope with them in building a new tomorrow. My vocation in life has been to try to mend broken marriages. With the cultural change since the last generation, I have witnessed a shock wave striking at the heart of our social structure—the family. I want to help you understand your marriage and yourself. I want you to learn to develop a close relationship and a relationship that allows for growth together and growth as individuals. Rather than to moralize or to speak in platitudes, I have chosen to make concrete suggestions. I am interested in what you are doing. Success in your marriage will come about through action, through the way you behave. That is what Reality Therapy is all about.

Recently we have seen a wave of nostalgia for the "good old days" of the 1930s and 1940s. Music, plays, books, movies, comics and even clothing styles have been revived to remind us of times when life was easier and simpler. You could always count on the Model A Ford to get you where you wanted to go. It was a rugged, dependable car. It was easy to operate and repair. If something went wrong, there weren't a lot of decisions to make about what the problem was. Today it takes a highly skilled mechanic to analyze and repair cars loaded with sophisticated equipment. Now Ford advertises its Pinto as a "basic, durable, economical car"—a return to a simpler way of life.

Human relationships, too, have become more complex. This book is designed to help you cut through these complexities. You will be offered practical ideas that will work if you are willing to work at them. Anything worth doing requires planning and effort and a bit of determination.

Most of the recent books about marriage deal largely with the topic of sex. Many readers have found this approach fun and interesting. I don't want to demean the importance of sex, nor will I criticize the many techniques and the prolific amount of information that have been made available; neither do I intend to add to this volume. Sex can be exaggerated to a point where it becomes dull. Nothing can be more boring than a pornographic movie. After the novelty has passed, these films usually drone on monotonously. After you've seen all the different ways of having sexual relations, that's all there is. No plot; no story; no human dimension. The same can be true in marriage. After a couple has sex in all the different ways there are, they still have to get along with each other. That's what I want to talk to you about—interpersonal relationships. If you want to learn how to live together creatively, this book can help. If you want a manual on sex, you will be disappointed.

As you are reading, please don't agree or disagree with what I say. Just think about what is said. Let the ideas kick around in your mind. Discuss them with someone. Try some of the suggestions. After that, read it over again. As you attempt to put these ideas into practice, many of the ideas will be more understandable. But it will take time and more reading to fully benefit from this book.

Any good interpersonal relationship must be worked at. I have a very good friend who is a most attractive woman although she has never been a cover-girl beauty. She once told me that while at college she was always the last one asked out in the dorm. She decided that when she did go out on a date, she would have to continually work at the relationship. This realization that a relationship needs constant work has, I am sure, been the major reason for her happy marriage.

All relationships—and especially marriages—run into problems. When the honeymoon is over, life becomes real. The possibility for happiness with another person lies not only in your ability to solve problems, but in the actual process of working together creatively in the development of a relationship. It is in the very act of thoughtfully, cooperatively and voluntarily working out ways to grow closer together that people find each other. This is what makes a marriage successful. It is not just what a couple does or has done; it is the process of "doing" wherein you can find and keep a deeper sense of love.

Sometimes we encounter problems that seem strong enough to tear any marriage apart, but they don't. Why? Other marriages seem vulnerable even to minor problems. I feel that if the couple's basic relationship is weak, any problem may present a major difficulty. If the couple's relationship is strong, they can weather the adversity and even be brought closer by it.

If the problems of a marriage are placed above the relationship itself, then priorities are misplaced and the relationship is vulnerable. If the relationship is strengthened and the couple grows closer, they are able to work at their problems without threatening the marriage. The stronger the relationship, the easier it is to solve the problem.

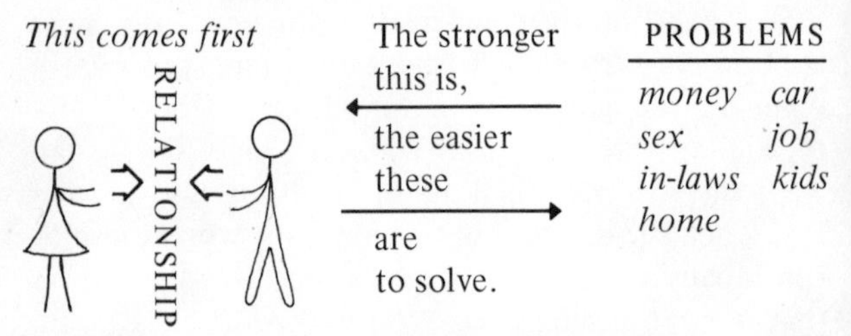

If the focus is on the relationship, then the problems will ultimately be solved. Developing a close relationship is needed to build enough strength into the marriage so that the couple can handle the responsibility of solving their own problems. For ultimately, that is what they must learn to do.

If the focus is on the problems, and the relationship is still weak, then the problems will tear the marriage further apart.

Working on problems can be a way of strengthening the relationship, but this is somewhat difficult and should be undertaken carefully, with much thought and work. This is what I shall talk about.

This book has been written for those who are committed to learning how to make a marriage work. You will learn to create alternatives and to construct successful pathways toward building a growing and deeper relationship. There are no games to play, nor do I offer instant solutions to problems. What I have to say takes time, lots of time. It takes work, lots of work. But the result—your relationship—is all worth it. I believe you will find many of the ideas presented here new and interesting. You will learn to view marriage, the most intimate of interpersonal relationships, as a challenge to be approached creatively.

A young girl came to my office recently who was concerned about her forthcoming marriage. "So many of my friends are having problems in their marriages that I wonder if it is all worth it," she said. Then she added, "There must be a better way; why marriage?" This book is an attempt to answer that question.

Chapter two

Woman's changing role

Woman's rapidly emerging new role has brought a multitude of changes in the husband-wife relationship. Her increasing awareness of the value of a woman's worth partially reflects this change. The whole thrust of the woman's liberation movement is their assertion that woman has more value as a person than man thinks she has, as demonstrated by the way he has treated her.

However, woman has always been more person-oriented than man. Over thousands of years her responsibility for childbearing as well as the major responsibility in the rearing and socialization process of her children have developed within her a greater consciousness and sensitivity to the wants and needs of others. A woman seldom does things just for the sake of doing them. More often than not she does things for someone, thus demonstrating this awareness of a person's true value. How much of this awareness is natural and how much cultural, I don't know. What is important is to keep all this in mind as we examine what is happening to her.

Today's women have more opportunity than imagined even a decade ago. Never before has she been so free of burdening responsibility. The woman of the 1970s may find her identity and fulfillment in many other ways outside of the family and the home.

Not many years ago the family was a unit of economic survival. In the Middle Ages, a man went out to fight as a warrior or to hunt or farm. The women stayed home. In our colonial times, the men tilled the soil and ground a living out of the earth; but still most women remained in the home. After the Industrial Revolution, the husband still left the home, but this time to work in the factories for twelve or more hours, six days a week. Women remained in the home. The full burden of maintaining the home for many thousands of years has been the woman's. Upon her fell the major responsibility of caring for the children and the home.

Today, however, many women have been reluctant to consider themselves exclusively homemaker, mother and wife. In the 1930s the vast majority of women were satisfied with this domestic role. What happened?

First, let's look at what women do today that is different. It appears that most women have the same basic need for love and recognition that they have always had. What has changed is how they meet these needs. Most women at one time found their identity and their sense of love and worth exclusively through their role as mother, wife or homemaker. The need to be involved with other people was met through social activities at home or church.

Not long ago the vast majority of a wife's time was spent in the home with the drudgery of cleaning, laundering, cooking, washing dishes, ironing, and taking care of the children. There was precious little free time remaining in a week's schedule. What little leisure there was was mostly focused on church or club activity. A woman's time could be viewed like this:

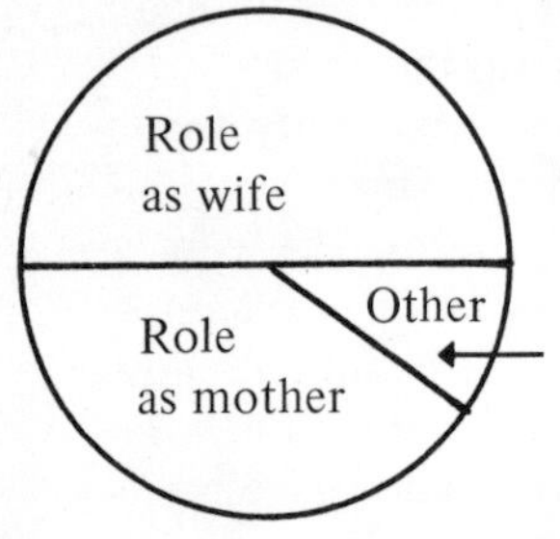

Even here many women found a role which largely was connected to her husband's job, such as belonging to the grange for farmers, or a women's auxiliary of her husband's lodge or a group in their church.

Before the age of modern conveniences, a woman's work was never done. In their preoccupation with "busy-ness," wives found much worth and identity. They found fulfillment and satisfaction in seeing their children eat foods that they themselves had canned and preserved. Children wore clothes made by mother's hands. The wisdom or motivation of this seemingly austere life style is less important than the fact that, up until this point in history, few women have had much, if any, leisure to think about. Home and children were their job, their leisure, their total life.

The significant change began after World War II with the age of gadgetry and appliances. Dreary household tasks like washing dishes became simplified by automatic dishwashers. Ready-made clothes that were permanent press relieved her from those many hours once spent over a hot iron. Dusting was reduced by furnace filters. Pre-packaged frozen foods eliminated the canning and preserving of foods. Vacuum cleaners, electronic ovens, automatic washers and dryers (remember the old clothes line?), "carry-out" dinners from the Colonel, Teflon, self-cleaning ovens . . . you name it. In a few short years the role of women had changed drastically. A significant amount of free time became available. Men, too, had a bit more leisure, but the change for women was dramatically more significant. A need for an expanded identity and ways to fulfill her need for worth had to be found. The "new life" brought little fulfillment for the woman who opened a box of frozen food–in contrast with her predecessor, who utilized her creative talents and skills in preparing homemade dishes. In short, women began to feel a certain emptiness and sense of inadequacy in their mother-wife role.

Smaller homes made less work. Disposable diapers further freed mothers. Television became a babysitting device. On and on into change, the work that was never done became almost disconcertingly manageable. The rhetorical question put in a TV commercial, "What's a mother to do?," has innocently signaled a serious inquiry into women's values. New questions are being asked. New issues are emerging.

I do not in any way wish to diminish the vital and busy role that a wife and mother still plays. My purpose here, however, is to call attention to what has changed and how this radical change has and will affect our lives–and above all, what to do about it.

A woman's time can now be viewed as:

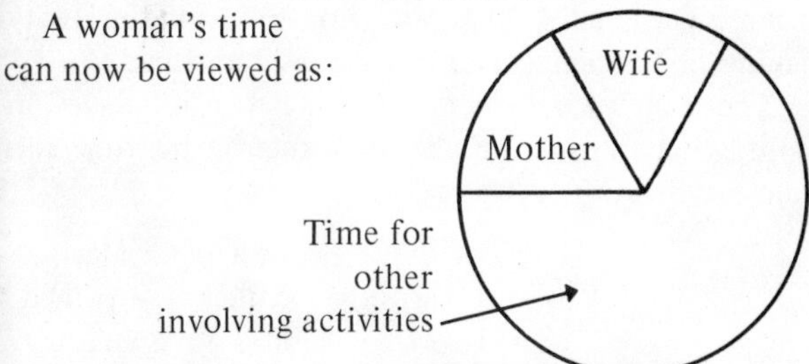

A woman's basic need for love and worth (one cannot exclude men from these needs) through involvement still remains, but she must find fulfillment in different ways to react to the opportunity and to respond to the change.

Many women are now working in business and industry. Whether to augment income or avoid boredom, the result is the same–a significant change in traditional family life. At the same time, dependency for financial security has begun to diminish. Financial security, once the central consideration in a prospective marriage, is now at least secondary. One young working mother whom I counseled recently put this whole idea rather succinctly. She said, "Money won't make you happy. It'll only make you more comfortable when you're miserable."

The economic liberation of women is interwoven with their newly found opportunities in employment. Divorce is more readily an acceptable alternative to a woman when she is not faced with economic destitution. Women are now competing effectively for a wide spectrum of jobs, and the occupational opportunities are expanding rapidly and not just for menial jobs as once was the case. More and more women are entering the professions of medicine and law. Many modern women look to marriage as a way to have a satisfying personal involvement rather than ma and pa playing house. The quality of the relationship is undoubtedly taking preeminence over other considerations.

The trends I have been referring to can be seen in comparing the average age of women at the time certain events in their lives occur. For example:

	Marriage	Having last child	Last child in school	Married women staying at home
In 1930	22	33	39	70%
In 1970	20	26	32	30%

Since most women are having their last child earlier, this again gives them freedom at an earlier age. How to use this freedom becomes a question of paramount importance. It has caused women to reevaluate their goals and pursue more personal fulfillment. Many have found they want their fulfillment in career identity. As she climbs higher and higher in academic studies, woman wants to reach in ever-widening directions and be given the same chance as her male counterpart to do so. She wants the chance to make a choice of either staying home and having children or doing something else with her life or a combination of both.

The career could be as a volunteer (if she has someone supporting her or enough money in the bank) or as a professional in the business or service field. My own wife, along with raising eight children, has taken a very active and responsible role in various challenging and worthwhile volunteer organizations in our community. Not only has getting out of the house broadened her horizons, but it has made her own life far more enjoyable and fulfilling.

I know countless numbers of women whose own life includes their family and a professional career. Many counselors whom I have known find the career and family combination most satisfying. One good friend of mine, a happily married woman with three children, is doing an outstanding job as a school administrator.

Other women I know have chosen not to marry, but rather to direct all their energies in some professional capacity. I know of a woman social worker, for example, who heads the social services department of a large hospital. Katharine Hepburn chose acting as a career over marriage—not because she disliked marriage, but because she felt she couldn't do both and acting appealed to her more.

More is expected of the marriage itself. Women no longer view a marriage as being successful if the couple just manages to get along and remain together. Now marriage is seen more as a shared relationship. The doing of things *together* becomes important. Each person expresses a need for self-expression and growth. Roles are flexible and interchangeable.

Marriage became a more colorful experience for women when they no longer saw it as a denial of self, where self-identity was almost totally sacrificed to the demands of home and husband. Women also wanted more from marriage than just a nice house and healthy children. Even a second car is not at all important to a woman in relation to the current central issue—to be married to the type of person with whom she will find joy in sharing the adventure of life. This is not to say that much of life does not remain the same. But there is a significant shift in the ranking of priorities for most young women whose life styles have changed from that of their mothers.

Another important concept in understanding the changing role of women today can be best explained in allegorically viewing a woman's availability in what I will call "the marriage marketplace."

The term "marketplace" is used to refer to that time in a woman's life when she is available and receptive to marriage. In other words, during this time a woman is looking for a man. She may be in no particular hurry and she may be very choosy; nevertheless, she is "in the market" for a man.

Since there are fewer men than women available for marriage, women in effect are "competing" for a man. The number of men is less for a number of reasons, such as prisons, homosexuals, and the armed services. The market is somewhat imbalanced and it is well for a woman to be aware of it.

If for any reason she withdraws herself from the marketplace, intending to return later, she will find the going tougher than before. The reasons are quite simple:

1 As time goes on, there are fewer men available because of her age.

2 If she has worked, gone to school, and done things that in her eyes increased her own self-worth, then her standards for the kind of man she wants are considerably higher. Of course, the higher the caliber, the scarcer the commodity. In this discussion about the marriage marketplace, I am applying laws of economics, like availability, marketing, and quality.

3 Another basic reason why it is harder for a woman to find a man later in life is that the available men of high "quality" have also increased their estimation of their own self-worth.

When a girl is between eighteen and twenty and assuming she is moderately attractive, it is much easier for her to get married if she so chooses. This is prime time for finding a marital partner; and the longer she delays, the less are her chances—especially if she is constantly increasing in value in her own eyes.

The rapid increase in the rate of divorce places many women back into the competitive marriage marketplace. No-fault divorce laws are now in effect in several states. When this law went into effect in California, the number of divorces increased from 73,000 in one year to 107,000 in the next. In New Jersey the total rose from 14,000 to 26,000 in one year. These divorced women will face a greater imbalance when they return.

Another fact she must face is the increase in practice of living together without marriage. The premise of "Live life to its fullest and enjoy yourself" has prompted many young people to put off marriage while they pursue the "singles game." There are at present 48,000,000 single adults in the United States, and 12,700,000 are between the ages of twenty and thirty-four. This is a massive 50% increase since 1960 for that age group. The number of women under thirty-five who have been divorced but have not remarried is now at 1,300,000. This is more than double the figure of a decade ago. With permissiveness in sex, it's hard to move a man to marriage. Also, I believe the biological instinct of man to get married is less than woman's.

Yet another way of living together is the trial marriage. The purpose of a trial marriage is to find out if the marriage will work out by living together as if you were married. But if you are living together, no matter what you call it you are married. You are just not as married as if you were formally married, that's all.

The stronger the commitment, the better the chance of the marriage sustaining itself. Just living together to see if things will work out just doesn't seem to make couples work as hard as when they are legally married. A few marriages do seem to work in this arrangement, but then I believe most of these would have worked out anyway.

Also, the purpose of going together (sometimes called engagement) is to see if there is enough common interest to sustain the marriage. That is the time to find out how the marriage will go. You haven't cut loose all ties with others.

Another point is that the girl is the greater loser in the trial marriage since she goes back into circulation with less chance for remarriage than before.

Some say the economic and sexual liberation of women has opened other avenues for her to find personal fulfillment. In spite of trends, marriage remains the statistical norm. But affluence and change in goals and opportunity have persuaded her to reject settling for any old match. She will hold out and hold out, hoping to find a man of higher and higher quality. If she is willing to live with a man without any commitment, she has removed herself from the marketplace with little assurance of marriage. If the relationship is terminated, she returns to the marketplace with less chance of marriage, and her male companion with a greater chance.

She should be aware of these imbalances so if she does find an acceptable partner, she will handle herself in such a way that a lasting and rewarding relationship will develop. For a man, sexual involvement is easily begun and easily terminated without any sort of commitment. A woman today must be able to handle this challenge. She must creatively and thoughtfully find as many ways as possible to develop enjoyable and interesting experiences for them to share, while at the same time limiting her sexual involvement. If a man experiences difficulty in becoming involved with her sexually during their early relationship, he will either leave her or she will take first place in his eyes. If he leaves, she had little to hope for anyway. If he stays, he will begin to assume some responsibility for the depth of the relationship, thus committing himself to working toward more involvement.

The problem of understanding and building involvement through commitment is further complicated by yet something else; namely, man's tendency to have a distorted sense of his own value. I believe magazines such as *Playboy* have contributed to this. These periodicals seem to make their money on reinforcing the distorted value of the male, while at the same time downgrading the value of a woman to nothing more than a sexual object. And when a woman does become an easy object to be taken for granted, it is hard for a man not to get an inflated ego when sex is readily available without his working too hard to do anything which would say to a woman, "I come to you with some value, not just as a man."

It is easy to understand how a man developed this disproportionate view of both himself and women. Ever since he has been able to see and listen, he has been constantly reminded and exposed to this overemphasis of woman as a sexual object, not only by some magazines, but by most of the media, especially advertising.

Finally, anytime there is a market disparity (which I mentioned earlier), anything that is in short supply gets an unrealistic value assigned to it and thus, as a man finds himself in this situation, his distorted sense of value increases even more.

Thus, for a woman, she should somehow communicate to the male that she sees him for his true value, not his distorted value, along with her attempt to increase her own sense of worth and her commitment in the relationship.

This building of a commitment is extremely important. The easier it is to get out of a marriage, the less inclined people are to commit themselves to work at their marriage.

Since the advent of no-fault divorce laws, I believe, people have become less and less willing to work at their marriage. Women especially should keep this in mind as they begin to develop relationships, because ultimately they have more to lose.

Women have indeed changed and with the change have come new problems and difficulties. But face them she must if she is to find a happy marriage.

Chapter three

Modern man

While the role of women has been undergoing drastic change, something has been happening to the role of men. Throughout recorded history, man's primary goal has been to survive. In our day this is known as earning a living. First survival, then security. Our breadwinner's life has centered around his occupation to such an extent that even his leisure activities are often spin-offs of the job. Numerous social activities, such as sports, lodge, and professional groups, are directly associated with the occupation. Such pursuits sometimes enhance prospects for success and promotion. The goal is to achieve a position with some measure of affluence and security. Secondary goals are the marriage and family, and such pleasure and hobby pursuits as travel, sports, and home workshops.

Even in the very recent past, the priorities of the man of the house were as follows: first, earn a living and attend to those extra things to secure and improve the job; second, enjoy the fruits of your labor. A man's wife was expected to give him the moral support and physical comfort essential in fostering the career. As the reward for effort improved, so did the family's life style. Her happiness was conditioned by his happiness and success.

At social parties, but less so today, one might find all the men congregated in one part of the house talking about sports, business and politics. The women are gathered in another area talking about children and fashions. Not long ago the segregation of the sexes was even more pronounced. Golf and bowling leagues were all male or all female. Men might go on fishing trips or even on vacations without their wives. After all, the good man works hard, makes a living for the family and deserves a rest. When I worked in a steel mill during the 1950s, it was not uncommon for men to go fishing in Canada with their buddies or take a hunting trip to the Dakotas. I remember a group of men acting surprised when I mentioned that I rarely went anywhere, much less vacation, without my wife, because I considered her very much a part of my life. A man selected his wife to fulfill her role as homemaker, sex partner and mother of his children. However, something has been added. Now a man will tend to think of his wife more as a life companion. Segregation of sexes at parties, lodges, and vacations alone, have given way to more conjugal activities.

Today a man's idea of enjoyment will center more around his wife and family. Understanding this significant change is important. In marriages where couples still pursue a segregated social life, disagreements and frustrations are likely. In addition to seeking a partner, a woman now expects a man also to be a companion. There is a hoped-for maturity wherein a couple will share their lives in every phase and intimacy.

If a husband goes to his bowling league two nights a week, stops a third night at a local bar, goes to a lodge or a club the fourth night, and expects his wife to stay home, he will be asking for trouble. Women today perceive marriage as a sharing of lives. Not many years ago a woman might have spent lonely nights at home while the breadwinner sought his own diversion. Women were taught not to expect much more from marriage. The husband was all-important.

As the work week was reduced, men had more time for leisure. There was more time to spend with the family. The need for "companionship" between husband and wife now takes preeminence. Much to the dismay of some die-hard men who still think of their wives primarily as sex partners and mothers, the wise young husband-to-be will find a wife with whom he has many things in common. The socializing process of interaction between a man and a woman now should play a very large role in partner selection. Women expect a marriage that has an authentic and involved relationship. No more just the cook and dishwasher. In marriages where this turn to maturity has not taken place, trouble is likely.

More and more, man is going to have to face the problem of adapting to the increased amount of leisure time. The following diagrams illustrate the expansion of leisure during the past thirty or forty years. The reason for the earlier focus on work is evident. The

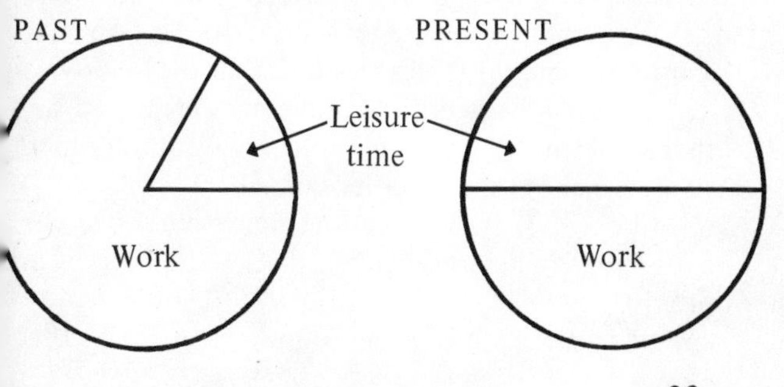

reason for change is also evident. Projecting into the future, the general trend of more leisure time will continue. Some economists have predicted that by 1984 most men will work a twenty-four hour week.

In years past man derived his basic sense of worth and fulfillment from his job. Status and prestige in the community hinged upon his position in the community's occupational hierarchy. A man with ambition and drive would strive to fulfill his unmet needs by climbing an occupational ladder to success. Only then would the community acknowledge and respect him. Dignity was essentially associated with a man's occupational pursuit. This was so very important to the man of achievement that he came to view what he did in his job as the most important aspect of his entire life. His wife shared this view for many reasons. Her role was to keep her husband happy. Also, as her husband progressed through various social and occupational ladders, she and the family were also accordingly afforded more prestige and opportunities. So the husband and wife worked toward the common goal of progressing occupationally, which was the same as succeeding economically and socially. A man's job took precedence over his marriage. His dutiful wife understood her role and accepted it.

The increase of leisure and the new role of women has added a challenge to marriage. Today, if a marriage is to endure, both people have to develop similar interests and do things together that they enjoy. A woman now sees herself as someone capable of another self-identity besides her role as wife and mother. Today a man must take a look at where his priorities are and decide how his relationship with his wife will be affected by his job or his activities and friends, or both.

What frustrates many ambitious young men is that

they often make a success of their occupation but they can't simultaneously make a success of their marriage. The goal can be achieved but the prize lost. What we must understand is that today the criterion for success has changed in the eyes of society. Success is no longer found in a career alone, but now co-equal to and often more important is a loving, rewarding relationship with his wife and family. Men and women derive a sense of worth, fulfillment and identity from different sources. It is no longer just the job, but it is the family relationship that determines his happiness and success.

Husbands now do tasks that heretofore were considered woman's work. Here is another key to understanding change. What is so different about many of today's marriages is that there seems to be ever-decreasing boundaries and separation of household and marital duties defined by sex. Young people have been brought up to see that if a job needs to be done, there's no difference who does it as long as it gets done. There is less means of identifying a marital job with the sex of a person.

Women washed the dishes simply because it was a woman's job. Men had such tasks as cutting the lawn or washing the car. I remember our first night after the honeymoon. When we finished dinner, I went into the living room to read the paper. My wife washed the dishes. It never occurred to me to help her because that was *her* job. These role-connected jobs seem to be disappearing. Modern couples tend more to teamwork. Frequently the wife will also have a job. The mutual sharing of lives and doing things together without set formulas is another sign of change.

Many men have adjusted to this changing life style and its new criterion for worth and success. Some find it quite rewarding, while others prefer the traditional marital job distinctions based upon sex. The more conservative person prefers definite roles within the marriage. If a man of traditional tendencies does not choose a wife with closely similar attitudes, trouble is in store for the marriage. Such a person should be aware that most women today will not be willing to accept what was once the traditional arrangement.

Conditioned by a competitive society, the modern American male is among the most aggressive in the world. This aggressiveness, coupled with new business and industrial policies, such as frequent transfer to different cities, plays an important part in contemporary life. To most husbands a job move is a promotion and challenge. But many person-oriented women feel hurt by the insecurity and lack of roots which can result from these moves. Although many women learn to cope with these disruptions in their own lives, it is most difficult for them to adjust if the marriage and family are not very strong and close. Some place the husband's career first and accept the consequences. This is reminiscent of the traditional role of a woman. Many women now reject this idea. Today it is not unusual for a wife to tell her husband that she is not moving. These situations place severe stress and strain upon a marital relationship. I know of a woman who returned to college after her children were all in school. She graduated with a pre-law background and then was accepted into a law school in another state. She announced to her husband she was going there and placed on him the responsibility of figuring out what he and the children were going to do while Mommy went to law school.

As I mentioned earlier in this chapter, man's priorities have changed since World War II. Many have come to view their jobs as secondary to their family interests. Although they are still interested in occupational careers, they want to have a fulfilling and satisfying job—not one in which they merely earn a living. That's the major difference that has taken place in one generation. Although physical characteristics haven't changed much, today we enjoy better health because of medical progress. But the resulting vigor and longevity are most often used to find happiness in life and to do worthwhile things, as well as to earn a living.

We have learned to conquer much of our environment, almost to a fault. We dominate our planet and our dreams of spaceships, ridiculous only a generation ago, have been realized. Leisure is ours! The task ahead is to adjust responsibly to this incredible change. The task is to bring *quality* to our lives and our relationships. For modern man, figuring out what to do and how to do it is more than enough to keep him busy.

Chapter four

You can't change people

How your life works out depends largely on your point of view. Your basic outlook affects how you interact with other people. You are what you are. What you are will determine the tone of your interpersonal relationships.

Some of us accept our friends, lovers or marriage partners as they are and do not try to change them. I believe you will find this type of person cheerful, well-adjusted and happy with life. There is an element of acceptance and contentment here. This does not mean that such people are lacking in drive, ambition and motivation. When you are willing to accept life as it is, you are better able to master and control your own destiny. The opposite kind of person is often pessimistic and critical. Those who await utter perfection as a precondition for response will obviously find it difficult to have anyone to respond to. They try to change everyone with whom they come in contact, from their lovers to their business associates.

An essential basic step toward a successful relationship with any person is to recognize that we must learn to accept the other person as he is, with no strings attached. Trying to change someone as a condition to an authentic relationship is not a realistic way of life. It is trying to live in a dream future of one's own making. We are all far from perfect and indeed this is the beauty, not the weakness, of humanity. It is only in our fragile and imperfect condition that we need and want and love each other. We are all lovably incomplete.

I'll give you an example of what I mean. Carol and John came to see me as a marriage counselor, at her mother's request. Both were willing to discuss their marriage to see if they could make it a better one. They were quite anxious to talk openly about things. Carol began by saying she had known about several little habits of John that were irritating to her; but, like many people, she felt that once she was given the chance she could change him—always for the better, of course.

The person on the receiving end of such criticism seldom sees things in the same way. John said Carol hadn't wasted any time in setting out to reform him. It was hard to get him up and moving in the morning. His taste in clothes was poor. Just little things like this. Shortly after they had been married, Carol bought him some shirts and ties. She put them in the closet to surprise him. A nice idea, she thought.

John came home after work one evening and Carol waited for him to find those new ties and shirts she was so proud of. John saw them but didn't respond in a very positive manner. He casually mentioned to Carol that he saw the new ties and shirts and that it was nice of her to think of him.

Carol was pleased. So far so good, she thought. But the next day, John wore one of his old favorite shirt-and-tie combinations. Carol was frustrated. She began by telling John he didn't look as nice as he should because he always wore those same color combinations. John said he liked his clothes. After all, he had picked them out. He was comfortable with them. John stood firm in this conviction that he would wear what he wanted. Carol did not pursue the matter, although she was disappointed.

This was the first little disagreement for Carol and John in their marriage. It had resulted in some subtle disappointments for each of them. John felt Carol had become picky all of a sudden. Carol felt she was just trying to help him to improve.

The second little incident in their marriage came the following week when Carol decided that John should get up earlier so there would be less rush in the morning. Carol told John about her idea. John agreed there was probably some wisdom in this; although, he said, he always found it difficult to get up in the morning. But he agreed that it might even help his career if he got to work earlier. You know, get the jump on the day's work; possibly impress the boss; maybe even get a raise and, after a while, a promotion. John decided to try to change this aspect of his routine.

The outcome was not as noble as the ambition, because John's efforts at getting up early didn't last long. Evidently he hadn't impressed anyone—at least not himself. After several weeks, he had reverted to sleeping in and renewing the rush. Carol admitted she was peeved. John felt guilty that he was disappointing Carol. He was a "P.M." type of person and just couldn't seem to permanently change his behavior.

Enough about John. What about Carol? John said there were also some things about Carol that he hadn't liked when they were dating, but he had decided to overlook them. After they were married, her little habit of biting her fingernails irritated him so much that he decided "for her own good" he would help her to overcome this annoying habit. Carol admitted this habit of hers was unladylike, and that she had tried since childhood to stop biting her fingernails and couldn't.

John's plan was a simple one. Every time he saw her nipping her nails, he would simply call it to her attention. He did this with almost a reverence for duty. After awhile, Carol grew irritated. She began to ignore him with "righteous indignation." John thought perhaps a more vigorous course of action should then be taken. He decided to slap her fingers every time she put her nails into her mouth. With that, Carol began to grow hostile. She thought he never minded before. Carol resented this infringement upon her personal rights, and some rather harsh words were exchanged on several occasions. Although when they started on the correction, which both agreed was desirable, Carol didn't appreciate John's slapping, even though it wasn't hard. The plan just wasn't working.

This is a simple example of the ways in which one couple tried to change each other. In some marriages, these subtleties become major hurdles that hinder the future of the relationship.

It is impossible to have inner peace of mind when fretting over the human frailties and faults of someone you love. If perfection is a condition for a happy marriage, that is a higher price than anyone I know can pay. Some people have another word for trying to change people; it is called "frustration."

The only person you *can* really change is yourself. We tend to make value judgments about others that, in effect, result in criticism. Marriage is such an intimate relationship that there is a great deal of opportunity to criticize if one chooses to be a picky perfectionist.

It is the very act of trying to change a person that often results in tension and conflict. "I'd like you better if——." Is that really true or are we using what the other person is doing as an excuse for our own behavior? True, married couples have certain important responsibilities to each other. If one partner is doing something that may actually be harmful to himself or herself, the other does have the obligation to point it out. However, each mature person should be responsible for his or her own life's decisions.

Responsibility in a marriage is the ability to fulfill your own needs for love and self-worth while, at the same time, not infringing on the right of your mate to do the same. This is an important concept. It is fundamental to the building of loving relationships and to attaining worth as a person. What I am trying to establish here is that if your marriage is to be a happy one, you must accept the responsibility for what *you* can do and allow your partner to work at the marriage according to what he believes he can do.

You can't do the work of your partner. Each must do his own. Each must decide what to do and do it. Marital happiness is the involvement of two people, each of whom can fulfill his own needs while allowing the other to do the same. To repeat, *you work on what you can do and let your partner work on what he can do.* It is in the working at something that happiness comes, not in the reaction of another. The reactions help, but you can't depend on them or you will surely be disappointed.

Marriage is not an individual effort. Neither a one-sided love affair nor a one-sided marriage is ever successful. Marriage is a mutual effort. The idea of accepting others as they are requires maturity. Fairy tales ending in "They lived happily ever after" are for children. The process of accepting others is an ongoing task. Just like life itself, people grow and change and the marriage, too, grows and changes.

Marriage is a shared relationship. It is never one-sided. If it is, someone is stultified. What can *you* do to make your marriage better? What can *you* do *specifically now*, in the present, to have a better relationship? You must recognize that if you are 10% wrong and your partner is 90% wrong, you can only work on the 10%. You married a human being, not some idealistic perfection out of a Hollywood movie. So figure out what you can do. It's the only thing you can work on. I will suggest several specific steps that you can take, now, to make yours a better marriage.

The goal is to work at making yourself a better person to live with. A positive action plan may set you in the right direction. I call it a "Do Plan" because what you do must be something positive. Negative plans don't work. People who drink say they are going to stop drinking. That's great. But ask them what they are going to *do*. Not drinking to an alcoholic leaves many hours with nothing to do. The question should be, "Yes, I believe you want to stop drinking; but what are you going to do?" When you stop doing one thing, you have to start doing something else. And whatever you do is your "Do Plan." To the child who runs, say walk or sit down. To the person who is eating, say go for a walk (or go to Weight Watchers). To the drinker, getting active in Alcoholics Anonymous and their activities is a good "Do Plan."

Remember, regardless of what your partner does, your control over whether or not the marriage succeeds comes only from what you can do. If your partner isn't working at what he can do, that's his responsibility. If he doesn't assume that responsibility eventually, I see little hope for a happy marriage.

It is extremely important to realize it *is possible* through your own efforts in working at what you can do that you will help to influence your partner sufficiently so that ultimately he *may* choose to begin working at the marriage himself. By working at the relationship you make yourself more attractive and thus you make working at the relationship easier for him. But the decision as to whether he works at the marriage is still his.

But whether he does or not, you will begin to realize what working at a marriage is all about. And you will have done all you can do.

To begin working at a marriage, first try to establish a conducive mood. Let's call it "PMA" for "Positive Mental Attitude." Your state of mind is vital in getting the right start. Sit down and relax in your favorite chair, preferably when the house is quiet. Think about some specific behavioral changes you can make to improve your marriage. Behavior here refers to those things you do, those things over which you, yourself, have control. It is important that these things be specific, realistic and of short duration. They should be things that you can, in fact, accomplish.

For example, you say, "I can be nicer to Fred. That's it. Tomorrow I'll be nice to Fred all day." Although well-intentioned, you have programmed yourself improperly. Being "nice" is not specific enough. Being "nice" really is vague. The first rule: Do specific things to make your marriage better. Be realistic. Pick out manageable things you know you can accomplish, and within a limited time frame.

Also, make sure the plan can be easily repeated. It

should be something you can do each day. This way you establish a good habit pattern instead of a bad one. For a man to kiss his wife and thank her every time she bakes banana cream pie is fine, but that type of plan would be seldom used and would do little for a marriage. It is important that whatever we do, can be done regularly, every day.

It is a sound principle in psychology that we can accomplish tasks more easily if we know precisely what it is we intend to do. Make the task possible and plan it for a limited amount of time–an achievable goal. We now call this a "success experience." It means simply that when we accomplish the tasks we have set out to do, the success provides reinforcement and encourages more possibility for growth. It is sort of a cyclic process. Success brings more success. The closer the reward is to the task completion, the better is the psychic gratification you receive.

Here is a plan developed by a wife who was seeking to make her marriage work. Judy, an elementary schoolteacher, decided there were specific things she could do every day that would make life a little more enjoyable. She thought that since she got home before her husband, Tom, that when he came in the door after work each day she would give him a kiss, smile and say, "Hi, handsome." These were three specific behaviors Judy planned. They were realistic, of short duration, and she knew she could accomplish all of them and they could be done regularly. *No matter how she felt, she would do them.* The greeting as two people meet, or a smile and a kiss between lovers, all help to establish a mood. The initial five to ten seconds when people meet each other are crucial in setting the climate or tone of the relationship. Judy's plan was simple, direct, realistic, repetitive and could be accomplished in a short period of time. It was something she enjoyed doing, and he appreciated her focus on his arrival. Judy later decided to have the house in order and to be attractively dressed. Each of these plans was added, little by little, over a period of a month. The important thing was for her to succeed, so she was careful not to take on too much at any one time.

Being a "giving" person makes it easier for others to be "giving," but doesn't guarantee their reaction. All of this is kind of like setting off a chain reaction.

Why not make a plan of your own? List one or two specific things you can do to make your relationship with your husband or wife a better one. Write a note. Send a card. Give a flower. Smile at the breakfast table. These are all ideas. Remember the ground rules: Be specific; be realistic; be certain you can accomplish what you set out to; and make it for a short duration and something you can do every day. And remember, you can change yourself, but you can't change anyone else.

Chapter five

You can't understand others

One of the four basic "can'ts" in any relationship, but especially in marriage, is that no one can really fully understand another person—and it really wouldn't help much even if we could. We have been living in what is often referred to as the era of Freudian psychology. This discipline claims it is important to know *why* we behave the way we do. Many professional counselors spend hours with people in therapy as they relive the past to ascertain the reason for their present behavior. The Freudian's goal is either to control or change what the person is doing with his life. The scientific principle here states there is a reason for everything. These reasons can be identified and explained. Following that logic, knowledge about ourselves can be categorized. Consequently, we can be labeled; and once labeled as paranoid or schizoid, we can understand the present and future behavior. All behavior is influenced by past events. First explain the cause and then proceed with the treatment.

From my perspective as a reality therapist, I believe that human behavior is too complex to be easily probed and labeled, and further, that it really isn't necessary. People constantly defy the so-called laws of predictability as based upon their background. What I really want to question is why we should spend so much time being concerned with the past in order to understand the present. And once we have done all this, all we know is why. We still haven't dealt with *what* to do.

Very often a marital spat will bring on an agonizing appraisal of the past to seek blame, to find cause and, I presume, to unravel all the knots of the past to create an understanding of the present and a hope for the future. You and I know this is not how the building of a happy relationship works. Knowing why something happened doesn't in itself change anything. All a person knows then is the cloudy why. Rehashing over and over is a waste.

I want to deny three points: (1) that it is important to find out why someone does the things he does; (2) that a person can be happy with another person only after finding out why he does certain things; and (3) that it is possible to know definitely what causes certain behaviors. The modern concepts of Reality Therapy dispute older premises of human behavior or psychology of the human mind.

What really counts to a reality therapist is what people are doing, not the reasons why they can or can't do things. Some people have so many excuses it would probably take a lifetime to sort them all out and to determine which are real and which are not.

In a marriage, especially when it isn't working as well as it should, the excuses become innumerable. For instance, look at this range of typical excuses.

WHY MY MARRIAGE ISN'T AS GOOD AS IT SHOULD BE

EXCUSES EXCUSES EXCUSES EXCUSES EXCUSES

Blame my health
I've had this terrible cold . . .
I have migraine headaches and . . .
I'm tired all the time because . . .

Blame my nature
This is the way I am.
I can't change.
I have always been like this.

Blame others
His mother is always . . .
Her girlfriends keep . . .
The kids always . . .
My foreman is . . .

Blame why
If I only understood why she . . .
I can't figure out why he . . .
Why do we keep fighting . . .

Blame feelings
My nerves are shot.
I feel lousy.
I always get upset when . . .
I'm depressed and . . .

Blame my partner
She gets me upset when . . .
He makes me feel bad when . . .
She never cleans the house . . .
It is either TV or sex, that's all he ever wants.

Blame something
The damn faucets leak and . . .
The car never starts and he . . .
Her sweeper is . . .

Blame past
She was . . . and has been that way ever since.
I've never been lucky. Nothing ever goes right. I've never been successful.
No one has ever liked me for myself.
My other marriage was just as bad.
My mother used to beat me so . . .

As soon as a reason is found, then that reason becomes an excuse for the behavior. That excuse, in essence, absolves the person from the responsibility for what he is doing. Until we begin to accept the responsibility for what we do, we will continue to feel worthless and will never draw close to anyone.

Whenever people stop thinking about what they can't do and why they can't do it and begin to think about what they can do, they begin to make a better marriage.

The reason people live their lives filled with excuses is because they fear punishment. The more concerned people are about just survival and security, the more effective punishment is. Excuses were the means by which you avoided punishment. If a husband comes home late from work, to avoid the punitive action of his wife, he makes up an excuse like, "The boss held me overtime" or "I had a flat tire."

Excuses absolve us from acting in a responsible way. All of us excuse ourselves. Just try living one day of your life without giving any excuses for anything you say or do. If you can do this for a month, it will have a profound effect on your life.

Another reason for giving excuses is the fear of a loss of friendship and respect from those we love. We don't have enough faith that the relationship will sustain itself without an excuse. We are concerned that without an excuse, those we love might think less of us or they might eventually reject us. Couples who don't have to give an excuse for what they do have developed a high degree of trust and respect for one another.

For instance, what if a wife takes the new family car to work and somehow bangs up the fender pretty badly. She brings the car home. When she gets home, the husband may be upset about the fender, so having an excuse about why the accident happened or how the fender got banged up is thought to be an easier way out.

If she went home without an excuse, the husband may say, "Why did it happen? How in the hell did you do it? Why . . . ?" and so on.

This all causes hardship, malcontent, and a lot of upset in the marriage. The car fender causes trouble between the couple. The loving feelings between the two people will, for a while, be rather negated all because of a banged-up fender.

It would be much better for a person to come home and be able to say, "I banged up the car fender. I made arrangements to get it fixed. I'm sorry I did it. Let's forget about it."

The husband, if he were attuned to not looking for excuses, and if he were living in the present and could accept things the way they are, should say something like, "Sit down, have a drink and relax. Come on. Forget about the fender," or something like, "Are you OK? Fenders can be replaced; people can't."

What a better world it would be if people would only remember that an excuse doesn't change things, and the reason why something happened won't make things any different from the way they are. While people agonize over reasons and excuses, they continue the type of behavior that continues to weaken their marriage and their lives. The basic idea behind insight therapy or psychoanalysis is supposed to give a person insight into his problem. Insight, whatever that means, does not change reality–the way things are now. Everyone must learn to live in the present, for the present is reality. The past is gone. The future isn't here yet. Living in the present is accepting life and not making excuses.

Each person, husband and wife, must begin to work with his or her own behavior. No more excuses. In examining a personal trait, it is not essential or even necessary to find out "why" someone does something. Excessive examination of a person can be both useless and harmful. Let us consider a specific example.

Betty was about twenty-two years old when she was referred to me by her family physician. She had been complaining of headaches and of not being able to sleep at night. She said she couldn't read for any length of time without getting a headache; and, in fact, she said she couldn't concentrate for longer than three or four minutes at a time on anything. Betty lived at home with her mother. She had never been married. Her father died when she was nineteen. Both she and her mother worked full time. Between the two of them they had a comfortable life, economically.

When Betty and I first talked, she said she had already been to several counselors. A specific physician's report accompanying Betty's referral said that no apparent physical reason could be given for Betty's migraine headaches and frequent insomnia. After having tried several counselors, Betty and her physician apparently thought she should try still another counselor. That's when she came to me. Betty said that each of her other counselors had tried to figure out why she had severe headaches. They had probed her past, her childhood, and her memories of her experiences in life. Her first counselor had concluded, according to Betty, that her sexual experiences had been so inadequate that her headaches were her psychosomatic reactions to her failure to find fulfillment in bed.

Betty's second counselor said her physical illness was a manifestation of her unpleasant relationship with her mother at home, and the earlier relationship with her deceased father. By the time Betty came to me, she was thoroughly confused. All she had accomplished after two years of counseling was that she had two different explanations why she was ill. Betty said she had analyzed her past so much that she was no longer certain as to what was fact and what was fiction. This is one of the tricks a tired mind can play on a person. Trying to recall the past with accuracy, as it really was and not as one might perceive it to be, is not a simple task.

In my opinion, what was important for Betty was what she was doing with her life in the present and whether she was satisfied with what she was doing. I spent no time analyzing her past. We started our counseling relationship on a different note than she had previously encountered. The first thing we did was to take a look at what she was doing in her present life.

Betty said she was a secretary in a large industrial firm. She wasn't too friendly with anyone at work. She did general typing and secretarial work for several different executives within the firm's main office. After work, she would usually go directly home. Her mother worked in a factory and the work schedules of the two women were such that they didn't get to see much of each other. Betty said the difference in the hours they worked made it almost impossible for her and her mother to be close and to share the interests of their lives. She wasn't dating anyone steadily. Many weekends she didn't go out at all. Betty spent her free time watching her favorite TV programs and doing things around the house.

After several conferences, Betty told me that she had broken off a relationship with an older man with whom she had become involved sexually. She felt that the relationship was not satisfying; that she had to end it, no matter how much it hurt.

I asked Betty about other close friends she might have. She hadn't kept in touch with many of her girl friends since they graduated from high school. She didn't even know if some of them were still nearby. Eventually everyone had stopped calling her, and she lost interest in calling them.

The first specific question that I asked her was simply whether she thought it would help her if she called a friend and talked to this person for at least one minute. She thought it would and agreed to try. Calling someone she had not seen for several years would not be an easy task. I had suggested the small time segment of only one minute because I felt she could do this. After Betty accomplished this first step, she confidently embarked on calling several other girls. Some of them were from her place of employment. Gradually the telephone conversations lengthened. Betty's friendships began to carry over between work and what had been her dull home life. She found this sociability to be increasingly enjoyable.

Betty now had to develop some personal interests, hobbies, outside herself—pleasures she could share with others and which would give her a sense of worth. There was one thing she had always wanted to do, and that was to refinish furniture. She even had an old bedroom set at home. Perhaps this was where she could start. We called a local school where adult education programs were offered during the evening. A course in refinishing furniture was offered at one of the high schools but not until spring. What could she do now during the winter months? A radio ad for skiing lessons caught her fancy. Her imagination was stirred and she had begun to develop a certain boldness and independence.

Betty had started to move outside her personal problems and toward other people. Later she decided that she should make more effort at bettering her relationship with her mother. Betty decided to wait up and talk to her mother several times a week. She began to help her mother with different hair styles. Her mother eventually responded by becoming much more open and talkative. This was a big change from the cold silence they once shared.

I gave Betty some alternatives on how to carry on a conversation. Many times we will ask questions that require only a one- or two-word response. The purpose of a conversation is to discuss things of common interest. It is best to ask questions of an evaluative type to draw out the other person. A few examples of such questions are: "What did you think about the play last night?" as opposed to "Was the play you went to last night good?"; or "Tell me what you thought about the music" as opposed to "Did you like the music?"; or "What's your opinion of the present administration in Washington?" as opposed to "Do you think the President is doing a good job?" The idea is to ask questions that draw out the opinions and ideas of others. Then you share your ideas. This is discussed in more detail in Chapter Ten.

Perhaps through the development of this one segment in Betty's life you can see why I believe that it is important to deal with present behavior, what the person is actually and presently doing in his life. Knowing *why* people do things seldom helps. In the intimate relationship of marriage it is too time-consuming and most often useless for one partner to try to understand why his partner does what he or she does. The love relationship between two people is based on *caring* and not on understanding why.

Many married people love to agonize over why they do something. While they agonize the "why" they continue the type of behavior that strangles their marriage. Even accurate insight as to cause does not change reality—the way things are now. Learn to live in the present.

Married couples want a vital, successful marriage. A happy marriage is geared to living in the here-and-now. Even after years of psychoanalysis, people are not sure they know why they do certain things. Why conjure up the past if it doesn't do any good and if it isn't necessary?

Modern methods of science, psychology and Reality Therapy are guiding people's lives toward ways of increasing the joy of living together. The only thing over which you have any control is your own present behavior. What you can change in your behavior is that which you alone are motivated enough to change—or what you really *want* to change.

Each person, husband or wife, must begin to work with his or her own behavior. "If she'll have dinner ready on time, I'll be pleasant when I get home" is not the way to work toward improving a relationship. This example is still dependent upon the behavior of someone else. "If he helps me get dinner when I get home from work, I'll be more sexually attentive to him later on." Do what *you* yourself can do. Use your imagination. Make things happen by figuring out what you can do. Just look for what needs to be done, then plan a way to do it.

Accept the world and people as they are. Each morning when you get up, say to yourself, "I am going to do something worthwhile and see someone I enjoy." Plan a good day for yourself. Fill your day with enthusiasm and squeeze in some things you like to do. Beware of manufacturing your own unhappiness by looking for the flaws in the people you love and those you meet. Better yet, plan to *share* your life and your day with those you love.

Here are some practical ideas:

1 Spend two or three minutes a day thinking of the good attributes of your husband or wife.

2 Compliment him or her when he or she does something you like. It's easy. Just say something little, such as, "That's a nice outfit you have on," "You know, it's fun being with you" or "You did that really well."

3 Don't be afraid to compromise! Individual selfishness has to be surrendered for mutual gain, especially in marriage. Accepting others and "doing your own thing" was never meant to mean the exclusion of mutual respect for each other or failure to meet the other person halfway. Nor can it ever mean the domination of one over another.

4 Forget about trying to understand *why* your husband or wife does something. Think about what you yourself can do to make things better. If petty irritations get you down, remember that the irritation is in you, so it is up to you to figure out what to do to get along with the irritating person.

5 Try doing things for the one you love just because you love him or her. Expect nothing in return. See what this does for your marriage. Remember, it is in the very act of working at getting along with someone else that you yourself begin to change, mature and grow. The payoff should not be how others react to you, because people's reactions are often erratic and rarely reflect what you are trying to do.

There are many things I do for my children which bring little or no immediate reward from them. The agony of a father telling his daughter she can't date when she is fourteen, then hearing his daughter say, "I hate you!" as she runs to her room crying, brings him little immediate reward. But if the father has enough strength and confidence in what he is doing to withstand the present pain of his daughter's reactions, he will enjoy the satisfaction of having made what he thought to be the best decision because he loved her. It is easy to do things that bring immediate rewards and praise from others, and much harder to do things you know are right when no one is applauding you.

6 Discuss this book and my specific suggestions with your husband or wife. There is much wisdom in talking things over together. Constructive discussion always brings two people closer together. Later I will discuss in more detail how married people can talk to each other and get increased enjoyment out of it.

7 Constantly work at improving your marriage. Determination is vital. Marriage is a venture of partnership, and both partners must work at the growth of their personal relationship as well as at their growth as individuals. Do what *you*, yourself, can do to make things increasingly better. The spirit of love, of life, and of giving of one's self in a relationship is bound to grow if both parties seek this. Your marriage can be only what you want it to be, through your own loving effort.

8 Finally, don't give up. All this effort at improving your marriage takes time, and I mean lots of time. All change is slow. So remember–*never give up*.

Chapter six

You can't make people love you

We all want to be liked and admired. There's nothing wrong in that. It is very normal. You might hear a person say, "I don't care whether anyone likes me or not." You know this isn't really true. It is human to want to be loved.

However, no matter how hard we try, we can't force people to like us. TV commercials have been trying to tell us that if we use a certain type of deodorant or toothpaste, we will be sexier, healthier, happier and more popular. If this were true, divorce courts would have all but gone out of existence. Those who deliberately seek love from someone who doesn't feel the same way about them seldom find the relationship to be lasting or even attainable. Even if they are able to develop this sort of love with another person, it is extremely difficult, under forced circumstances, to maintain a genuine, sincere loving relationship. It is up to you to love your partner and it is up to your partner to love you. Love is simply something that cannot be forced upon another person.

Of course, one must also recognize that certain basic human kindnesses and courtesies greatly help people to endear themselves to others. Some people naturally seem to do things that make them more likable. Learning to get along with other people is a vital and sometimes difficult aspect of human behavior. Sometimes the desirable relationship between two people just isn't there, no matter how hard either person tries to make it happen.

Let us consider the following example of an attempt at a forced relationship. What happened to Mary Ellen, a client of mine, when she was confronted in her marital relationship with her husband, Ben, is probably a good example. Mary Ellen and Ben had been married for about ten years when she began to reflect on their marriage. She thought about how their relationship toward each other had changed during the past ten years. She said she loved Ben and wanted to keep their marriage going. In fact, Mary Ellen was doing everything she could think of to make Ben love her. She cooked his favorite meals; she did whatever he wanted on weekends; she never nagged him about the fact that he played lots and lots of golf. She even had tried to please him sexually.

She said they used to do everything together when they were first married. She said they used to have many common interests. They liked to go to plays and movies together and with their friends and neighbors. They even used to shop for the groceries together. But somehow their relationship had gradually changed over the intervening years. It was a gradual, unnoticed change. Mary Ellen was convinced that she wasn't the one who had changed. She still wanted to do things with Ben, but she said that Ben seemed to be growing more and more indifferent to their entire relationship. Ben said he was just too busy at work.

He had become very successful in the sales field, and he said he just didn't have time to take her to a lot of places. At night Ben said he was too tired after working all day. He said Mary Ellen wanted to do things like play bridge with some of the other couples in the neighborhood or she would want to have some friends over for coffee.

Mary Ellen was bewildered and said she simply couldn't get Ben interested in anything that had once been so enjoyable for them. About a year after she noticed this change, Ben asked Mary Ellen for a divorce. That's when she came to me for counseling. Mary Ellen said she was miserable. Ben refused to discuss things either with her or with anyone else. He had moved out of their home. What could Mary Ellen do? She was torturing herself with all kinds of questions and self-doubts. She was rehashing the past over and over again. What could she do to save her marriage? What had she done wrong? The answer in this particular case, in my opinion, was that she had done all she could do. She didn't realize that it takes two people to make a marriage work. The relationship between them, although it had once been there, had apparently dissipated over the years. I believe it probably could have been brought back if they *both* would have been willing to work at it. But as long as Ben would make no effort at reconciliation, there was actually little or nothing Mary Ellen could do beyond what she had done.

There are many people in the United States who are getting divorces when one of the partners does not want the divorce. The other day as I was driving home and listening to the car radio, the announcer on KDKA in Pittsburgh said there were ninety-five divorce cases in the court system on that particular day—August 1, 1973. I am sure that if we were able to talk with each person involved in these ninety-five cases we would find that not every person wanted a divorce. We would probably find some cases where some people still loved their partners, but that the other persons no longer cared about them and did not want to continue the marriage.

Occasionally some people try to use things like gifts, money, and sometimes sex in order to gain love and happiness in a relationship. All of these things are only temporary; they can bring about a superficial love between two people, but it seldom endures. The aftermath of this sort of relationship can sometimes be traumatic, to say the least, if it results in marriage. A marriage based on a foundation of this type takes a lot of effort to keep going.

I believe there are some basic, sound, and simple fundamentals of human behavior that successful people exhibit rather constantly. These are the pleasant traits that make them so likable to others. For some people these traits seem to come naturally. Others must put forth a lot of effort toward being likable or sociable. Those who make this effort sincerely want to have more friends. They work diligently at improving and maintaining their relationships with others. Authentic human involvement is not an easy process. It requires work. Life and love are sometimes compared to a garden: You have to keep working at them or the weeds begin to crowd out the flowers.

The willingness and desire to work at a relationship is the first step to bettering your interpersonal relationships. Any person can enjoy the companionship of others even if he is shy, retiring, or hard to get along with. If he has the desire and is willing to work at a relationship, he already brings to the relationship the potential of success. In fact, reality therapists believe that one of the ingredients people need to be happy is to recognize they need people. It is not what others can do for them that is needed, but people need others to share in things like friendship. People need to lead worthwhile lives and do worthwhile things in the eyes of others as well as in their own eyes. The feeling of not being wanted or needed is one of the most devastating of all human psychological emotions. The "loner" is just that, lonely. It is never pleasurable to feel lonely or to lack the experiences that can be shared by two people, friends, or husband and wife as they move through life together.

Although everyone needs to show affection, achieving it is another matter. To some it comes so easily. How do they do it? To others, the harder they work at it, the further it seems from their grasp.

A middle-aged woman once complained to me that she didn't feel well. She said she didn't have any friends and that no one cared about her. "What can I do?" she asked. It never dawned on this woman to ask herself, "What have I done today to try to make someone else happy?" Happiness comes *not* from looking inward but from looking outward, a reaching out for life. Happiness is achieved through reaching out to others and, through this process, developing authentic involvement with others. It is in doing things with and for others that happiness begins to come.

If you look at successful, happy people, can you see one trait they all seem to have in common? I believe they all have a keen ability to relate to others. They all seem to have many friends. They have happy marriages. They are involved in various group activities not just for status but because they enjoy people. They enjoy what they are doing.

Look at successful marriages you have seen. Are there similarities in them? The chances for success in a marriage are overwhelmingly improved if both people work at getting along together. Many couples do work hard in the early years of their marriage. Sometimes they must . . . just to survive, to get established or to become successful financially, and to bring up their children. It is usually after they acquire most of the things they desire that something begins to happen between them. Usually they quit working at the relationship. After many years of being married, they think they can take each other for granted. They have reached a plateau in their relationship. They really aren't moving toward each other. Their relationship is no longer growing. Sometimes when the couple is at the summit of the mountain, at the top of the ladder, or when they have "made it" through the hardest of times, they begin to have marital problems. Sometimes when couples arrive at the top of success, they have then felt some overwhelming misery in their marriage. Their marriage seems to fall apart.

Why? I think it is because love is a continual process of involvement that needs constant attention. You can't ignore it and expect it to still be there when you want it. Love is sharing and working together along the way—all the time. Love is not like putting money in the bank where you can go and get it when you need it. Many couples look back and reminisce about "the good old days" when they were starting out on a budget. They laugh about the fun they had together. Actually, it was not the money or the times or the place where they lived. It was a time in their lives when they really worked together and made a lot of efforts at making a success of their marriage. It was the very things they did together and for each other that they should examine and recapture. When both people are trying to get along and are thoughtful of each other, it is much easier for them to draw close to each other.

When people stop working with and thinking about each other, the marriage begins to get into trouble. A noted psychologist has said that people should find their love relationship more reassuring when they can take their partner "for granted"; and when a couple takes each other for granted, they have established security and faith in each other. He concludes by saying that people must be able to take their spouses for granted in order to have a good love relationship. I disagree.

Stability, reliability, and knowing that the other person is there when you need him are essential to any lasting relationship. But this doesn't mean you stop being considerate and thoughtful of your spouse. An essential ingredient for any happy, successful marriage is constantly being thoughtful of the other person. That means *not* taking the other partner for granted to the extent that you overlook him or her because he or she is always there. It doesn't mean flowers for mom once a year because it is mother's day. It doesn't mean a package of golf balls for dad on father's day. It means you know someone loves you because they think about you and they show it rather frequently, if not continuously, by their actions. A person who really cares about someone expresses his love through caring. This is what involvement is all about. The willingness to reach out toward each other is an individual decision that each partner must make in the marriage. In everyday life perhaps one person can be a success, but in a marriage it always takes both persons to make the marriage a successful one.

Marriage is a shared adventure into life. If your marriage is not, then you must do what *you* can do to make it better. Remember, you have no control over other people as to how they behave. The marriage based on 90% of your efforts and 10% on your partner's efforts is still a marriage. If this is your case, you have some basic choices before you. You could accept the relationship as it is. You might even decide to have no relationship at all with that person. Or you might decide to work at what *you* yourself can do to make it a better marital relationship.

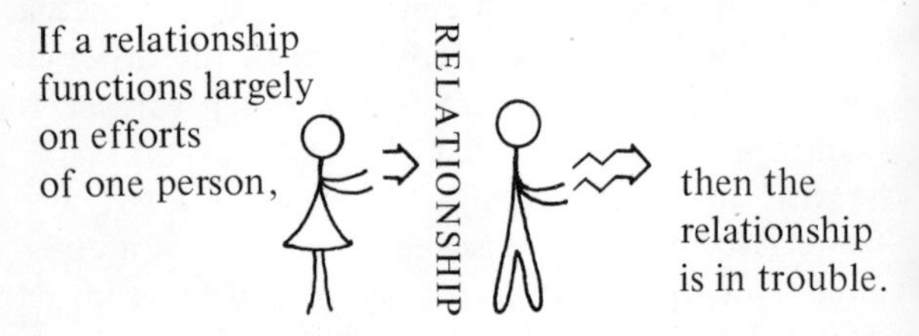

If you choose to accept a relationship like the last one shown, then you must work at what *you* are going to do *specifically* in your life and your marriage so that your life is a better one. Remember, it can't be a vague plan like saying you're going to be "nice." Plans and courses of action like that are too obscure; their chances of success aren't too good. A plan has to be specific and definite in order to succeed. You might also recall that we talked about making your plan a "Do Plan" instead of a "Don't Plan." Knowing what you are *not* going to do in marriage is not as important as knowing what you *are* going to do. Once you know what you're not going to do, you still have to figure out what you are going to do. That's sometimes pretty tricky.

For instance, if a wife says, "I'm not going to nag my husband anymore when he comes home," she has a perfect example of the "Don't" type of plan. That plan might be OK, but what is she going to do to fill that time when she no longer nags? She might say, "I'm not going to do anything then. I'm just not going to nag him when he comes home." The trouble with her plan is that when her husband comes home she will do something. She might choose to be silent and maybe not even talk to him at all. She might say she'll retreat to the neighbor's every day when her husband comes home. She figures that way she doesn't have to worry about what she is going to do.

On the other hand, she can develop a "Do Plan" of positive, specific behaviors like, "I'm going to smile when he comes home and ask him how his day was." Or she could say, "I'm going to smile and hand him a drink. Tell him to relax for ten minutes and I'll have dinner ready then." These last behaviors are examples of specific, positive acts that she could perform. They offer better alternatives than nagging or doing nothing. They are behavioral patterns which would enable her to enhance the relationship with her husband. They are things *she can do regardless of what her husband does* . . . no matter what mood he comes home in. And as she begins to focus in on her own behavior, to improve the relationship, she is doing the only thing she can do. As she begins to make herself more attractive by changing, it is up to her husband to respond. She can do nothing else.

Give the following ideas some thought. You'll find they can be relevant to your own life.

List two things you have done in the past two days to show your husband or wife that you love him or her. Be specific in this list. If you really want a challenge, try listing four different things you have done during the past two days to show your husband or wife that you love him or her. Do not repeat any item if you use this second step. Do this for a week. Remember, never repeat an item. You should make a different list for each day.

An extremely important point to remember when doing things for others, whether you are dating or married, is that it is in the very *process* of doing things for others that you begin to fall in love. It is also through the very *process* of doing things with and for others that you stay in love. The rewards and joys of any performance are always greater than the end product of that performance. The joys and rewards you will find in marriage are also found in the process of the doing and not in the expected goal.

It is up to you to work at what you can do to make the marriage a better one. You can't force others to love you or to be happy.

Chapter seven

You can't make someone else happy

Abraham Lincoln said, "We are about as happy as we make up our minds to be." In life what often determines whether or not a person is happy is his mental state or frame of mind. Happiness is an individual's attitude of being or his personal outlook on life. What we think is what we are. No one else can think about things for us. It is up to each of us to think and determine whether or not we are happy at any particular moment. All of us make these decisions every minute, every hour, every day of our lives.

Some people have searched for happiness for years, not knowing what it was they were really searching for. They thought happiness was a steady, blissful frame of mind where there were never any ups and downs. Happiness, as we'll see, is not a constant state of well-being. There are varying degrees of happiness. It is quite normal to feel a little low one day and better the next day. But the difference between happy people and unhappy people is that happy, successful people do not stay depressed for long periods. They know that it's common to at times feel happy or to feel depressed. It feels good to be happy, and happy people prefer feeling good to feeling sad. Happy people consciously make choices of behavior that bring them out of their depression.

In today's advertising culture, people are often misled by slogans which imply that happiness can be attained by buying certain products. Car dealers would have us believe that "Happiness is owning an XYZ automobile." Driving a certain kind of car, smoking certain brands of cigarettes, using a particular deodorant or a toothpaste will neither guarantee nor give anyone happiness. We know this, but we would like to believe we could be happy if we buy a certain product. It's easier. And if things make us happy, then the more things we have the happier we will be. But is this true? For to be happy a person has to do several things that take effort. He must first make a decision he wants to be happy, and then he must diligently work at his concept of happiness.

In marriage or dating, some people believe that they can make, help or force others to be happy. I once saw a parent spank his child for crying while riding a merry-go-round. There are people who mistakenly believe that buying presents for their husbands or wives or taking the "little woman" out to dinner is the key to a happy, successful marriage. Happiness is not a gift, a place, or going out to dinner. Happiness is neither found enroute to a place nor at a place, such as the advertising of the airlines or steamship lines would have us believe. Happiness is the result of involvement with people. In going out to dinner together, a couple finds happiness in sharing each other, in being together thoughtfully. In the *process* of doing things for each other, the husband and wife know that their partner is thinking about them and cares for them. By showing the other partner that you love him or her, you find happiness together as well as individually.

Each of us may be thrilled temporarily by something or someone, but lasting happiness must be worked at to be achieved and enduring. *It is in the thinking of what you can do for your partner and in the subsequent doing of these things* that you bring happiness to yourself and to your partner. The choosing of thoughtful, responsible behavior leads you to more involvement with your spouse and to happiness.

Many still believe that happiness can be bought or forced, and that ultimately they can "make" someone happy. It seems to be the easy, obvious way. A young woman may think that letting her boyfriend, her fiance or her lover get intimate with her will really make her man happy. It may thrill the man temporarily, but no woman yet has been able to keep a man happy for long by just offering him sex. That often comes as a total surprise to a young woman who has offered herself physically, and maybe rather often, to a man who, after awhile, says he is no longer interested in her. It is not unusual for a woman in a situation like this to do almost anything to hold onto her man. Happy, healthy sex can only be the reflection of an intense personal relationship. It can never be the cause of it.

The successful relationship two people enjoy is not based entirely or to a great extent on sex. A pleasurable sex life can help people build a better marriage, but sex alone will not hold a marriage together when everything else in the relationship is falling apart.

The husband who comes home carrying flowers and a box of candy and maybe even tickets to a favorite play or movie may still be in for a startling surprise. All these things may not make his wife happy. Human relationships and people just don't work that predictably. While some believe people do behave as predictably as counting from one to ten, history proves many of these predictions to be unreliable.

No one ever has control over whether or not others are happy. It is true that people can make it easier for others to be happy, but the decision is still an individual one for each person to make.

Many of my clients have told me they couldn't understand why their partners weren't happy when they had been doing everything possible to make their marriage a success.

One client caught up in the throes of trying to make someone else happy was Pete. When we first met, Pete was so perplexed about the unhappiness of his wife, Gladys, that he didn't know what to do next. He said he had tried just about everything. They had been married only six months. Pete said no matter what he did, it just didn't seem to be enough to make Gladys happy. She wasn't overdemanding, he said. It was just that anything he did didn't seem to make her happy for very long.

It seemed that their marriage had consisted of one little unpleasant incident after another. Gladys and Pete were the sort of couple who would talk some things over together. They were proud of a mutual agreement they thought of. They called it a "compact," after the famous Mayflower Compact where the Pilgrims agreed to talk things over. Pete and Gladys had set aside ten minutes a week when they would talk over their marriage and discuss how well they were doing. Pete said he was determined to make his marriage work. More than anything else in the world he wanted Gladys to be happy. He really went about working at it, too. He said that he had been doing everything Gladys told him to do during their weekly talk sessions.

Pete said that in their early talks Gladys had told him that if he would stop leaving his clothes all over the floor in the bedroom and bathroom she would be happier. It was a simple thing, really, and Pete said he complied with her wishes. He stopped leaving clothes scattered about their new home. Gladys said she wasn't going to be his new mother, who simply waited upon his every wish or picked up after him.

Pete said that during their third "compact" session, Gladys said she would be happier if Pete would just let her know when he was coming home late. She worked for a data processing firm and got home promptly at 4 P.M. every day. On the other hand, Pete was an auto-parts salesman. He had a large territory to travel and his working hours varied, depending on the day's events. He agreed that if he were going to be late in coming home, he would call and let her know.

But neither of these two changes in Pete's behavior made Gladys happy. There always seemed to be another and another item to be changed so that he could make Gladys truly happy. Gladys said his shoes were always so messy when he came home. His shoes had oil and bits and pieces of metal on them from the various auto body shops he had visited that day. Pete said this was just part of his job as an auto-parts salesman. During one of their weekly talks, they hit upon the solution that he should take his shoes off before he came into the house each evening.

Again, even after having accomplished all these things, there were yet other disagreements. One came when Gladys told Pete that he had parked his car over too close to hers in their double garage. She said it was too difficult for her to get in her car when she left for work in the morning. She said she would be happier if she had more room for her car. Pete replied that he needed a little more room in the garage so he could leave his shoes on a newspaper outside and not track up the inside of the home. However, Pete agreed that he could try to park his car over a little further to give Gladys more room for her car. So on and on went these minor changes between them. Pete was always searching and Gladys was never satisfied.

There were many other behavioral changes that Pete endured so that he could try to make Gladys happy. Gladys was the girl of Pete's dreams all through college. When he married her, he was determined that he was going to make her as happy as possible. What Pete couldn't understand was that no matter what he did, it was never going to make Gladys happy. Gladys had to make her own happiness. What Pete was trying to accomplish was impossible. Merely changing himself could never make Gladys happy.

In all relationships, a person should remember that he cannot force another person to be happy. Happiness, you see, is a decision each individual must make for himself.

Gladys began to change when she began to look at what *she* could do. And with this particular couple, the change came quickly. Once Gladys began to understand what she was not doing, her own awareness at what she could do began to increase. So did her happiness increase accordingly. As Gladys became happy, so did Pete. The two came together because they worked at their life together.

Chapter eight

Feelings and emotions

Today some married couples believe they have to talk about the way they feel toward each other and toward other people. They talk about relatives, friends and about everything. Some even talk about the way they feel toward the things their partner has done and is doing.

It is not uncommon today to hear, "Let's talk about how we feel toward each other." Or one partner may say, "Tell me how you feel about me today." This is a risky venture for any couple because they usually wind up discussing just superficial emotional feelings. The trend is understandable, for sensitivity training has grown in popularity.

At a time when you are feeling particularly tense, it certainly does not help to discuss the way you feel. Feelings are always hard to express accurately in words. Overstatement of fact is very likely to occur. The chances of misunderstanding or misinterpreting how a person says he feels toward another person are far too great. This sort of thing can be disastrous unless handled with care and consideration.

Let's take a deeper look at human feelings and see what is involved. First, the central nervous system is what makes a person different from all other animals. The human nervous system is a marvelously complicated network of nerves which works extremely well. It serves to tell you how you are doing. The nervous system works automatically in sending these signals to the brain, according to how we think or what we do. It might be pictured like this:

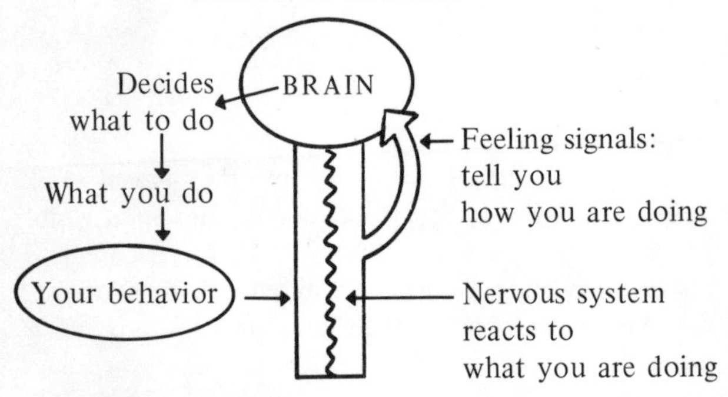

Suppose that a man becomes thirsty. The nervous system would automatically send a signal to his brain telling him about his body's need for water. If we would ask him how he felt, he would probably say, "I'm thirsty." This we call the feeling of thirst. His brain would then decide what he should do.

He might have decided to ignore the signal and continue thirsting. Or he might decide to get some water immediately. If he drank a glass of water, the signal or feeling he would then get is the feeling of pleasure which comes from a reduction or elimination of thirst. He has satisfied a basic need of his body. His brain would then decide that the feeling of drinking water was good.

Let's presume you are thirsty and have asked a friend for a glass of water. If your friend said to you, "Tell me about your thirst. How long have you had it?" you would think he was crazy. Here you are thirsty and your friend asks, "How long have you been thirsty? When did you first know you were thirsty?" You would probably respond, "What's with the questions? All I want is a glass of water."

Thirst is one kind of feeling/signal from the nervous system. When you're thirsty, you don't discuss it. Instead you act to answer the signal. For a married couple to discuss feelings like, "How long have you felt this way?"; "When did you first feel this way?"; or "How did you feel when I said . . . ?" solves nothing. The point is you don't ask a friend why he needs a glass of water. Will it really help when you ask your husband or wife why he or she feels a certain way?

When you are thirsty, you know why. And that doesn't solve anything. You still need water. Just talking about signals or feelings doesn't help. When the nervous system sends a signal that a person is depressed or lonely, *action* is called for. Behavior is the only thing that solves loneliness and depression.

Hunger signals a need for food. You act by eating. Depression and loneliness signal a need for people. And you must open up and get involved with others to fill that need.

It is a mistake to ignore the signal the nervous system sends to your brain. This is a valuable sign that tells you how you're doing. You don't ignore the signal of thirst or hunger. You act. In marriage you receive signals and feelings about how the marriage is doing. You feel good if your marriage is going well and you feel bad if your marriage is doing poorly.

To change the signals you have been receiving about your marriage, you must change what you're doing and thinking. This requires a certain amount of self-confidence. It is important to develop and maintain this confidence in your power to achieve a successful and happy relationship. It is at this point, when a couple lacks confidence that their marriage will work, that they should find a qualified counselor, someone who can help them regain the confidence and faith they once had.

One of my clients complained about her husband, her mother (with whom the couple was living), and even her employer. When I began to ask her about what she was doing to try to get along with these people, she thought for awhile, then smiled and said, "Nothing."

To begin to change himself, a person must first change what he is doing. Our behavior causes those little signals. To respond to the signal we must change our behavior.

Look at it this way:

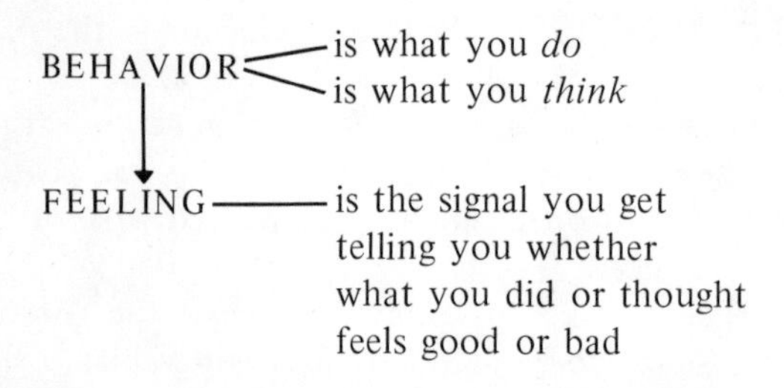

Behavior causes us to feel the way we do. The way we feel influences us to make decisions about what we should do next. Thus, the chain of events in everyday living goes like the following.

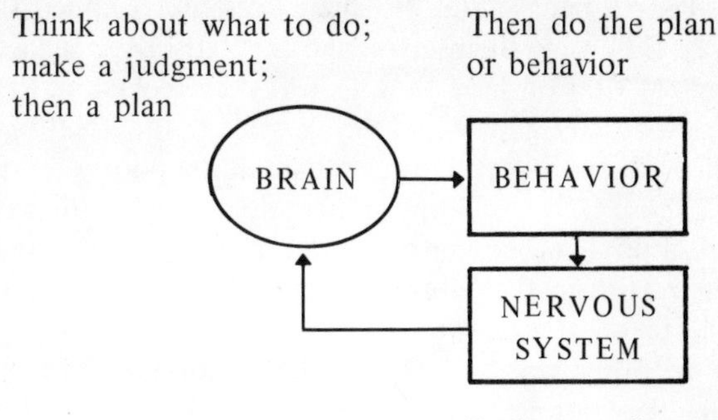

It is difficult to say which of these three functions comes first, but we can be sure that changing behavior will ultimately change our feelings. The feelings might not change right away, but eventually they will change as the behavior reinforces our thinking patterns and processes.

When you are thirsty, you don't sit around discussing your thirst. You get a drink. When you are feeling lonely or depressed about your marriage, you need to act. You need involvement with the other person who cares about you. It won't help to discuss your loneliness, indulging in self-pity. That can and usually does make things worse.

Getting along with others, and especially with the one you love, is a basic need for everyone. We might observe someone who is just hard to get along with and judge that he doesn't need anybody. That just isn't so. All of us have a built-in neurological need for other people. Those who have no one in the world they are close to do not really live; they exist. These are very lonely people.

People behave and live their lives pretty much the way they view themselves, and this self-image is based a great deal on how they feel. If they feel good, they are generally happy and doing well. If they feel bad, they generally feel failure and are doing poorly in life.

Those who are happy and are doing well in life have an ability and strength to tolerate temporary pain if their faith in the future is such that they believe they will feel better later on.

In other words, I can handle the disappointments and frustrations in the present if I believe the future is going to be better. Thus, if I have a disagreement with my wife today, I can handle it easily if I somehow have faith that our relationship is strong enough and I know that soon we will be happy again.

Those whose life is filled with failure, who have no hope for future happiness nor faith that things will be better, live only for the immediate feelings of the present. They have no faith that they will ever feel better in the future. They have no strength to tolerate the present pain because they have no hope in a brighter tomorrow.

Thus the alcoholic who throws liquor into his system is working for immediate gratification so as to relieve the present pain of loneliness, believing that there is nothing better for him in the future. He sees no hope in making any kind of authentic human relationship so he works only to eliminate the present pain of emptiness and boredom.

You will notice that the smiling, happy people are those who care about others and are involved. Involvement is always a reciprocal matter. We all like to be around other people who care about us and who are fun and pleasant. No one likes to sit in a depressive atmosphere and talk about unpleasant things. If a person feels badly, he feels badly. Talking about it merely reinforces his bad signals and prolongs and intensifies them. The kind of person we believe we are is the key to success in life as well as in marriage. Are you basically a responsible, worthwhile, happy person, or a lonely person who is experiencing failure? How I think about my wife or husband affects how I feel about him or her.

One man admitted to me he would awaken in the morning, look at his wife, and begin to think of all the irritating things she had done over the past week. All day, he said, he kept thinking of these aggravating things and by the time he got home, he would be in such a "rotten mood" he couldn't think clearly about himself or her. He said he felt "rotten."

I asked him to make a list every day of two good things his wife did the day before. He could not repeat what he had on the list from the preceding day. So each list was different. I also suggested that he begin his thinking of things for his list when he first awakened in the morning. Before long, he changed his whole outlook, especially toward his wife.

Appallingly, many of us look for annoying things to pick at everywhere, even within ourselves. It is up to *you* to change your behavior, the way you think about life . . . your attitude toward your husband or wife . . . your opinion of your marriage . . . your vision of life.

Rather than discuss the past, why not discuss what *you* can *do* to make things better. Formulate a plan for success . . . for involvement . . . for caring. Happiness is contagious. Smile and most people will smile back. Feel depressed or sad, and soon others around you are gathered into your depression. I had a friend who said that whenever he felt depressed and a cheery person would come around, he would try to do one of two things: get him depressed or get away from him.

We all have problems and concerns. How we meet them makes the difference. Whenever negative thoughts concerning your marriage come into your mind, try thinking positive thoughts. Negative thoughts cause negative feelings, and negative feelings almost always result in negative behavior for those who allow their feelings to guide their behavior. Generally, when we feel the pain of bad feelings, we let these feelings guide our behavior. When we feel good, then it's mostly our thinking that guides our behavior. We are not overwhelmed by painful emotion when we feel good so we naturally resort to thinking, which is how we are designed to behave. When we are relaxed and contented, then is the time to make plans as to what we are going to do when we get angry or upset. Then, as we feel anger coming on, having already thought out what to do, we put the plan into action. Thus, you do your thinking when it's easiest and, more importantly, when you are better equipped to make the wiser choices. When you feel the anger arising within you, you quickly put the thought-out plan into action. I'll go into more detail as to how to handle anger, but first let's review briefly what we have been discussing.

First, discussing negative feelings doesn't help to make a better relationship.

Second, common sense tells you to act when your nervous system sends a signal–like drinking when thirsty or eating when hungry or getting involved with others when you're lonely.

Third, don't ignore the important feeling/signals that tell you how you're doing. Everyone needs these signals to indicate where they are in life and especially how they are doing in relationships with others.

Fourth, to change the way you feel, you must first change your own personal behavior.

Fifth, incline yourself to the positive. Do things that are good and worthwhile for yourself and, more importantly, do things good and worthwhile for others. Marriage is a two-way relationship that both people need to draw on to feel good and sustain themselves. It is a unique relationship in its intimacy and sharing. Be sure what you share is positive.

A big problem in some marriages is fighting. Some say that fighting is good. "It clears the air," they say. Others claim this type of ventilation helps to get it "out of your system." Don't believe it! Fighting always hurts! It leads to exaggeration and distortion. The only thing you learn from fighting is how to fight. Fighting is the bottom of the negative spectrum.

Furthermore, fighting doesn't change things. It only moves people further away from each other. To change any relationship for the better, two people must move toward each other. Fighting is considered a super-negative behavior. It is what we do when our thinking no longer controls what we do. It is a way for our emotions or frustration to force change. Some of us may respond to this anger by changing our behavior quickly to avoid rejection from our marital partner. So we "take it."

On the other hand, some people, as an alternative to fighting, have conditioned their nervous systems to become depressed or anxiety-ridden. All of these feelings are in the negative category.

Those who have successful marriages are able to channel their energies more resourcefully. They may have just as much stress and strain as their angry neighbors do, but the difference is how they cope with problems—their behavioral responses. One of the first steps to happiness is learning what to do when you get upset or angry—learning to become the master of your own life. Sure we all get angry, but there are different ways to handle anger. Successful people learned very early in life what it was like to handle anger successfully. For example, they saw how their parents handled problems. They learned, through success experiences, how to be happy and thus how to feel good. This doesn't mean you "win 'em all."

All you learn from getting angry is how to get angry. I'm not saying that people don't have occasional fights in their marriage. All of us have experienced this sort of thing. If a person told me he never got angry with his partner, I would have difficulty believing it. Ultimately it is not how angry you get or how often you fight; it is what you can do to make your marriage happier that really counts.

What does fighting or anger really mean in a marriage? It usually means that one partner doubts his or her spouse really loves him or her. The hurt spouse says things like, "If she really cared about me, she would have been more thoughtful." The closer the relationship, the more it hurts when there is anything done which is interpreted as rejection. Thus, they feel hurt because in their eyes the other partner did something that hurt them. They reason that if their partner *really* loved them, they wouldn't have done anything to hurt their relationship. They hurt, and they want to strike back. They feel an urge for immediate action to force change. This is the scene that occurs when a woman throws something or the man slams his fist against the table. Perhaps she runs home to mother or the husband goes out for a drink.

Anger usually results in three courses of human behavior. One recourse is throwing things, either your own fist or the nearest object. Common sense should tell us that this cannot help. And it can hurt, especially if someone gets hit.

A second and more typical course taken in anger is yelling, screaming, or shouting. Some pretty nasty distortions and exaggerations are expressed this way. It is kind of an emotional enema that proves and improves nothing. People thoughtlessly say things they really don't mean. They criticize and "put down" each other.

Emotional stress is not relieved by striking out, verbally or physically, any more than extreme hunger pains are relieved by yelling and screaming at those around you. All the emotional stress tells you is that something is wrong.

The third course of action that many people take is to withdraw. The hurt person becomes sulky, pouty, or doesn't talk much, and is maybe totally silent for a day or two. He usually stays around because he's smart enough to know there's no use pouting unless someone is around to watch. On the job he may be delightful, but as he arrives home, Mr. Hyde takes over.

On occasion the pouter may feel so badly that he even temporarily withdraws from his friends. He can almost lose touch with reality. Anger is just a painful signal from our nervous system telling us that what we are doing is wrong. We should change what we are doing. But what else is there to do when we get angry? There are some sound, basic alternatives to anger which have proven to be successful for married couples.

One common technique of coping with anger is to change what we are doing into a positive course of action or behavior. One couple, whenever they felt angry at each other, would go to separate rooms in the house and do some physical exercises. Another couple I know would jog around the block together. The neighbors would say what a nice couple they were—they were so close that they even jogged together! Little did the neighbors know it was the couple's way of handling themselves when they felt angry at each other.

Usually physical action taken to handle anger is better when it is done apart. Most couples will find their anger attenuates faster if they take separate courses of action. One young newlywed couple agreed, after their first fight, from that point on whenever each of them felt angry, they would separate and do something else. This diversion acts as a behavior change and allows for a change in feelings.

Consider the case of Beth and Martin, both working as well as attending classes at a local university. I had known Beth prior to her marriage to Martin. Since their marriage, they had been fighting almost constantly. She had thrown so many dishes she had literally gone through two complete sets in three months.

In discussing this problem, I first asked Martin what he could do. He told me he had tried yelling and had sometimes tried the "silent treatment." I suggested an alternative of separating and going somewhere else, maybe just leaving the room and going into the bedroom. He claimed his wife would follow him everywhere in the apartment and they would continue the argument. Finally I suggested he should just take a walk when he couldn't control his anger. He liked the idea. He tried it, and said he lost three pounds during the first two weeks. Every time he got angry, he would go take a walk. He took as many as five walks in one day. Beth decided to scrub the kitchen floor as her change in behavior. She had the cleanest kitchen floor in the neighborhood. As they changed their behavior, their feelings then changed. When they cooled, they could come back together. Today they are happy. He is gaining weight and the floor looks ordinary.

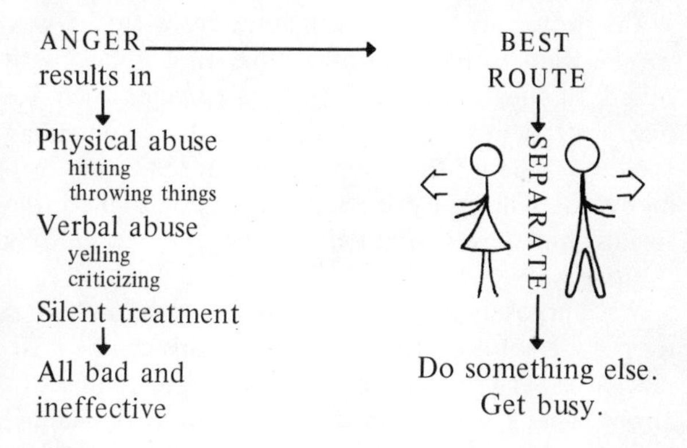

Anger does diminish in time. Some don't like to exercise or take vigorous courses of action. Some find exercise merely stimulates their mental and physical systems. The solution for these people is to resort to placid things like resting. If you are like this and find yourself upset, just go and lie down. Wait until you recuperate and feel better. You may want to go to sleep and wake up refreshed. One middle-aged housewife told me that she would take a relaxing hot bath whenever she felt herself beginning to get angry or upset with her husband or her mother-in-law.

Another husband told me that when he became angry, he would just say, "I'll see you in a half hour," and then he would go watch TV. It was his way of saying to his wife, "I'm angry. I'm upset. I can't maintain a good relationship with you right now. I love you and I value our relationship so I don't want to say or do anything to hurt you. I'll see you in a little bit when I feel better." His wife understood his anger and saw his behavior as a sign of his caring for her. Their relationship was much better. Such a technique ultimately helped resolve some of the problems they had in their marriage.

Emotions and feelings can interfere with the way people want to live, or how people want to deal with others, if they allow these feelings to guide their behavior. It is not easy, but the rewards are unending for those who let their thinking rather than their feelings guide what they do. Surely they don't ignore the signals, but they should look at *what they can do in a positive way.*

We purposely haven't mentioned "talking things over" as a solution to anger because this can be difficult. It is very difficult to talk when you are upset or angry. That's why courses of behavior that channel our actions to exercise or restful relaxation can result in gaining control of ourselves. They allow for positive reassessment of the situation. The best time for people to talk is when they are calm. Couples should talk about things that do not merely lead into another upset. *Don't dig into why* things happened or why you felt this way or that way. Better yet, don't discuss the past or your inner feelings. Generally tracing the cause will be of little help in solving anything. Once you know why, you know why–that's all you know. Looking back may only reinforce the problem. We come to a point where we must rebuild and continue to build a marital relationship. That requires a positive attitude and a look ahead.

Vicki and Jerry had an interesting way of solving their arguments or disagreements. They were both psychology majors in college. They were knowledgeable in their field, and they decided that every time they were on the threshold of an argument, they would separate for at least an hour. During this time they would each write down, specifically, two good things or behaviors that the other partner did. They included on the list what they thought they could do to make things better. At the end of the hour, they would meet in the living room for a meeting of their minds. They had a mutual understanding if they had not cooled off in an hour, they would meet and say, "I need one more hour." Vicki and Jerry kept up this arrangement until they were both ready to talk about whatever the crucial problem was. Vicki said that, as she sat there during the hour, she usually revised her list so that by the time an hour was up, there didn't seem to be too much really bugging her. What was left on her list she believed was important enough to discuss with Jerry. Furthermore, the couple derived a lot of value from compiling a list of possible behavior patterns that each could follow to make their marriage a better one. The emphasis in this technique is not on what is bugging you, but on what you individually can do to make things better.

The important thing to remember is to live in the present. Behavior is difficult enough to deal with in the present, let alone also dealing with the past. Even if you believe you can learn from the past, include what you are going to do now. If you believe you must talk about your feelings, relate them to specific behavior. It will aid you to focus on what will help. It is easier for others to visualize behavior than feelings. Marital relationships that are happy, successful, authentic, and rewarding are based on the things people do—especially the things couples enjoy doing together. Working at improving your marriage is easier if you work at improving specific behaviors. The way you feel will change as you change your behavior.

Chapter nine

How to change your behavior

How to manage my behavior?

How to stop?

What should I change?

How should I change?

Behavior is what you do. Each person is responsible for his own behavior. Each person decides what he or she does in life. Nobody can make the actual choice and decision for another person to change. Only you can change your own behavior. Although it is a fact that one can change his own behavior, changing is very difficult. The process of change is often erratic and slow. It takes determination to say, "I'm going to change what I'm doing." This chapter deals with some fundamental principles that, if understood and properly applied, can help you to change and improve your behavior.

Whatever it is that makes people want to change, the desire or motivation must be there for them to change. You have to want to do something bad enough before you change. A cigarette smoker with an occasional cough might not be motivated enough; let the doctor give him either six weeks to live or quit smoking and his motivation increases. It all amounts to the same thing: Personal commitment eventually must come before change will occur.

All of us have the ability to make a decision and carry it out through personal commitment. Some of us have learned this ability better than others. When a person has made a decision to change what he is doing, he has made a commitment. The steps to changing behavior are not complicated, but they do require work.

First you must examine what you are doing. You must ask yourself if what you are doing is helping you or not. This is a very important reflection that requires an honest response. Is what you are doing helping you or anyone else? This question should be extended to include whether or not what you are doing is helping your marriage. Is your behavior helping others or helping to make where you are a better place to live?

Look only at your present behavior. Refrain from looking at and talking about your feelings and emotions. Feelings tell you how you are doing; but that is all they tell you. To change your feelings and emotions, you have to take a look at the specific things you are doing in your marriage. Simply observe and note what you see yourself doing. Even then, you must be careful that you are accurately observing your behavior. It is like writing a movie script. You, the author, must actually visualize in your mind's eye everything you want the actors to do. And it is these detailed behaviors in your own life that you must see, examine and try to change.

Without the commitment, you won't even begin to look at the behaviors. And the commitment begins to develop and eventually grow stronger when, and only when, you have faith in yourself that you can do it.

In the case of marriage, a couple has to begin to believe and have faith in the relationship. Sometimes this faith first has to come from the outside, such as from a counselor, since the couple has lost this faith. To encourage a couple to work at this marriage, to have faith in their marriage, to see worth in each other and what they are doing is the job of the counselor.

Once a couple begins to have faith in their relationship by watching it begin to develop and grow, then the tough part of marriage counseling is over. For as you begin to see yourself do something successfully, you begin to develop an internal faith in yourself. But in any event, with or without a counselor, nothing will happen to the relationship until the couple begins to work at it, which calls for changing what they are doing.

Pick some small area of your own behavior where you really want to make a change. Be sure this is a small and manageable area. Most people plan big behavioral changes. After you have done this, make a plan of action. Don't program yourself for failure. Setting unrealistic, unachievable goals is programming for frustration and failure. Anyone who has a sincere desire to change can accomplish small changes. Making a decision and making a realistic plan are crucial to the success of changing.

Next you should be able to state specifically what it is you're going to do. Get a pencil and some paper and write down the change you want to make. Make the description detailed but also remember the change itself must be simple. Good counselors will tell you a sound principle of human behavior is to make one small behavior change at a time. Our goal here is to take a specific behavior and work at it. The success you receive by accomplishing the small change reinforces you to continue working at changing until finally you have really altered your behavior.

Be certain you have a positive plan and not a negative one. We have talked about this before but it is important. Your goals should be worded in a positive manner like, "Smile and give my wife a kiss." If you try to change by saying, "Don't be grouchy when leaving for work," your focus is on being "grouchy." Our minds work best when confronted by positive choices. If someone says, "Don't think of the color green," the first thing that comes into your mind is the color green. How about the schoolteacher who says, "Don't run, children, don't run"? All the kids can think of is running. Tell your friends, "Don't smile," and they smile at you. One word of caution. Any plan you make is made because *you* want the marriage to improve. If it is phony, either you will eventually become sincere or you will quit. Phony behavior doesn't last.

Next, establish a repetitive routine as a plan of action. Whatever it is that you are changing has undoubtedly been a part of you for some time. Change takes time. Good habits are slow to build while bad habits are difficult to erase. Choose a behavior you want to change that you do every day. For example, you might think of buying flowers for your wife on her birthday. This is great, but her birthday comes only once a year. Relationships between people occur on a day-to-day basis. Plan something that is specific, realistic, positive, and can be done regularly. Such a plan could be smiling at your husband as he arrives home at night, a call by phone once a day to say hello, or a special treat at mealtime of something he likes.

This is something very specific. It is of short duration and achievable. It is part of day-to-day living. Smiling and talking are simple; they are what friends do, and they are also behaviors that help make a marriage work.

Remember, changes in behavior can help to bring about changes in feelings. If you want to change the way you feel about your marriage, the way to begin is by changing *your* behavior.

To make any plan work, *you* must do it. A marriage plan for change that depends on *two* parties for its success is in jeopardy from the beginning. For instance, consider these marriage plans. A husband once said to me, "If she dresses up for dinner, I'll give her a kiss before we eat." Another husband said, "If she isn't in curlers when we go to bed, I'll be nice." One client said, "If he isn't so irritable, I'll be sexy," or "If he's in a good mood when I get home from work, I'll pour us a scotch." All of these plans are contingent upon one person doing something *before* the other person will change. The odds are stacked heavily against the success of these contingency plans. They are loaded with possibility for "cop-outs." Your behavioral change is based on what *you* do. Each person must concentrate on his own behavior.

Do not become upset with what your partner does or doesn't do; work at what *you* can do. We are all far from perfect. We all have a lot of learning to do. Marriage, more than most other human relationships, requires consideration and compromise. It should be a partnership in which individual selfishness is surrendered for mutual gain. It requires a great deal of patience and the willingness to never give up. The idea of "never giving up" is one that shows how much you care. Marriage has little room for egotistical self-centeredness. The need for change never ends in our lives.

To change behavior:

A The change should be small–in terms of time, in terms of what you do.

An example of time:

1 I am going to give my wife a kiss every time we reunite from now on. (too big a plan)
2 I am going to kiss my wife as I enter the house for the next two days. (good plan)

An example of what you do:

1 Be nice around the house. (too big)
2 Smile when you enter the house. Small success is what we want to achieve–success builds success.

B The plan should be made in detail. Talking about what you are going to do in vague terms leaves you an easy "out." Vague, ambiguous things never seem to get done. We have the illusion when we talk about what we are going to do we are already doing it. Plan in detail what you are going to do. For example, "Walk in the door, go directly to my wife, put my arms around her and give her a big kiss." You know what you are going to do. Writing it down helps you remember. When you write something down, it seems to have a greater force behind it. When you sign a note or mortgage on a house, you get the idea that you have to make the payment. Writing it down has an air of importance about it. People always write down important things.

The diagram below is helpful for many couples.

Example of specific behavior	Date 3	4	5	6	7	8	9	10	11	12	13	14	15
Kiss wife at night													
Start coffee in morning													

In this diagram, the husband checks only what he does. The wife checks only what she does.

C The plan should be positive.

For example:

1 Give wife a kiss.

2 Smile when I see her.

D Never give up. The result of what you do will be how much better you feel. Success experiences eventually condition us to be more receptive to change because we feel better. We must begin to believe that what we are doing is worthwhile. All of the good feelings which come from our successes help us to enjoy our marriage more and more.

Another plan one of my clients worked out for herself was:

A When I get up in the morning the first thing I think of will be, "I am going to do something worthwhile today; I am going to begin to look for good things to do and people to enjoy."

B Every day I am going to make a list of:

1 Two good behaviors my husband does every day. (Must be different behaviors each day.)

2 Two good behaviors I do every day.

A good time to change the way a couple feels toward each other is in the morning or when a couple reunites in the evening. These times help set the mood for the rest of the time the couple is together. If you start your day by saying, "I'm miserable; I hate life," a negative pattern is set for the rest of the day. If you give your wife a compliment rather than ignore her, this helps to start your day with a happier outlook.

Many people are "grandiose"–they want to do *big* things. They, in effect, set themselves up for failures. Ask yourself what it is that you are really trying to change. In an earlier chapter, we said that you can't change other people and you can't make them happy. What things can *you* change or do to make your marriage a better one?

Compatibility in marriage means that two human beings are willing to work at their relationship. They realize they are both far from perfect. They are willing to work at getting along. They are willing to share their dreams, their happiness, and their lives. Marriage is a giving of one's self intellectually, emotionally, sexually, spiritually—a sharing in all ways.

As we begin developing a relationship with another person, it is in the very practical procedure of figuring out what to do and then doing it that we mature and begin to change. Change for the better makes us feel good and conditions us to accept more change. Thus, as we take responsibility for what we do through creatively thinking about what we can do and then doing it, we are already beginning to open up to others successfully, forming authentic relationships. The loneliness that turned us inward begins to diminish. We develop a sense of worth and begin to feel good about ourselves and others. This applies to all of life's relationships, but it is especially essential to a good marriage.

Chapter ten

How to talk

Most of us find conversation to be a pleasurable part of everyday living. Talking does not require a lot of energy, especially when we talk with someone we love. Talking about things and thoughtfully interacting with the one you love most is one of the pleasures of married life. When two people come closer together in life, they share many things.

The key to talking is to talk in such a way that each feels free to express completely and openly all thoughts and beliefs to the other. And there is both revelation and satisfaction in really being heard. Talking, then, is expressing ideas, thoughts, opinions. To be pleasurable for both partners, conversations must include consideration. Two people come closer in their relationship to each other when they do not feel threatened in their posture of openness and vulnerability. What feels good is really the thoughtful interaction that occurs between two people. It is no fun to talk to someone who isn't listening. But when someone asks you a question and then listens thoughtfully to what you say, the joy of being with that person is increased. Part of the fun of doing things together and just being in the presence of someone you love is that the two of you are doing and sharing things you both enjoy. The spontaneity and joy of intimate conversation is fundamental to a good marriage.

Too many couples have forgotten how to talk with each other. Some never learned. They fail to communicate in a way that can be pleasurable to both of them. Hopefully at one point there was sparkle and fun in being together. At that time they couldn't wait to see each other and talk about the things they were doing and the things they might plan together.

Two people in love with each other, who talk to each other with such thoughtful interaction, actually reinforce their love constantly. They reinforce each other by listening, by being interested in the other person and in what that person is doing, as well as enjoying the things they are presently doing together or that they plan to do. Isn't that what couples do when they are dating? Successful relationships between two people are based on good communication. If these intimate conversations were important before marriage, then how much more important they must be after marriage. If marriage is viewed as a commitment between two people, then part of that commitment is almost total involvement with each other. Involvement means coming closer together. Couples who are warm and loving are able and eager to talk with each other.

The couples who have been married for some time, who find they can no longer converse with each other as they did when they were in the dating stage, have to take a long look at their present situation. What are they doing now that is different from the way they used to talk with each other? Perhaps that was as long ago as when they were dating each other or perhaps it never was.

This is a difficult reflective process. Many say they don't know what they are doing now that is different; but they conclude talking to their husband or wife isn't nearly as much fun as it used to be. Others simply don't talk with each other at all. There are many reasons why communications break down between people. The exact reasons will vary depending upon many factors in the complexity of all close interpersonal relationships.

Regardless of where we are in the spectrum of our relationship with another, there are some very sound, basic fundamentals that make talking more fun. That is what this chapter is about.

Talking must be done in the "presence" of others. This does not mean simply standing or sitting beside someone. It is much more complicated than that. The concept of "presence" in making talking enjoyable is vital.

The concept of "presence" can be viewed from three aspects: physically, psychologically, and mentally. The first aspect is physical presence. This is simple and obvious, but it is the reason talking is so much fun. Two people find enjoyment in talking together. There is little fun in being alone.

The second part of "presence" concept is to always talk with others in a psychological presence, which means you must be receptive to others. It means that you must be really listening as well as talking. It does not mean you talk and the other merely listens. It does not mean platitudes and put-offs. Any relationship based on this sort of behavior will seldom last very long. Talking means being psychologically present and available to the other partner. It means reserving judgment until what has been said can be thought about; it means getting away from a shallow type of listening and talking. Being picky, nagging, or fault-finding has a devastating effect on the conversation or dialogue. In fact, it almost always limits or immobilizes the ability of two people to communicate with each other.

An example of this immobilizing effect often occurs when two married people, obviously feeling they know each other very well, tend to react to what the other person does or says too quickly and judgmentally. Each little hurt tends to stifle future conversations. A woman might say, "I'd like to go out for dinner tonight." If the husband immediately responds with, "I don't want to. I'd rather stay home," he has closed the conversation. Since the wife had initiated the dialogue, it was incumbent upon the husband, if he did not want to go out to dinner that night, to offer some alternatives which would still allow room for the two of them to move together.

There are many other things he could have said in response to his wife's suggestion of going out to dinner. He could have offered an alternative like, "Let's go to McDonald's and then come home for dessert," or "Let's stay home tonight and go out tomorrow night." The options are unending, depending upon the ability to creatively think about other courses of action. These are alternate pathways allowing two people to continue to move together, and thereby reduce the possibilities of marital conflict. These alternatives allow both partners to more freely meet their needs. Marriages often succeed or fail in proportion to the extent that each partner allows the ideas coming from the other to be received and shared. Cutting each other down, or killing statements the other person has said, are dead ends in communications. In other words, you don't have to agree or disagree with what your spouse says. You can listen, think about what was said, and hold any reactions of your own until you have had a chance to think about the entire conversation. Marriage is sharing and this is what sharing means.

Imaginatively constructing alternatives always enhances a marriage and makes it more fun to be together. The more alternatives there are, the more chances there are for two people to enjoy each other. The important points in conversing successfully are: to be in the psychological "presence" of someone, to reserve judgment about what the other is saying and, in case of conflict of interest, to creatively look for possible alternatives. Getting along doesn't mean you always agree with what your partner says, but where differences occur the listener looks for and offers alternatives.

In essence, all good conversations are modeled on a four-step process:

1 Listening intelligently and thoughtfully to what the other person is saying.
2 Being nonjudgmental. Reserving judgment until the person has finished. For example, don't start shaking your head even before the person is finished with what he or she is trying to say. Reserve judgment until he or she has finished and until you have thought about the idea.
3 Don't rush. Allow time to think about alternatives that increase the ways you can enjoy conversation with others. This enables people to enjoy talking to you. Nobody likes to talk to the closed type of person whose manner is inconsiderate and at times threatening.
4 The last step is to act or move. If what is said is agreeable to you, then it is a simple matter to move

forward together in harmony and agreement. If you don't agree, then offer alternatives that still allow each partner to move.

In reality, people have three basic options in their conversations:

1 They either move away from each other through disagreement.
2 They move closer together through agreement.
3 They look for alternatives that allow each to move and for them to still move toward each other.

Two people cannot come closer together if they are moving apart because of some verbal disagreements. Creating alternatives is not synonymous with compromising; rather, it is the broadening of options. Many times alternatives turn out to be more enjoyable than the original plans. This is a rewarding and pleasant surprise.

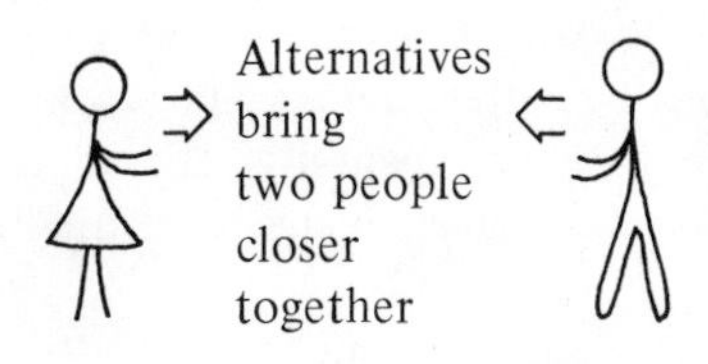

In addition to physical and psychological presence, there is a third aspect of "presence." It is mental presence. Mental presence simply means being mentally with the person who is talking *when* he or she is talking. It is surprising how many of us do not do this. A relationship is easily damaged when there is a lack of mental presence as partners try to communicate with each other. It means not considering them important enough to listen. There is probably nothing more cutting than to ignore a person face to face. On the other hand, mental presence means, "I hear you; I am listening to you; I understand what you are saying. I am with you and, most importantly, I am with you *now*."

Many couples don't listen to each other with mental presence. A husband may be listening to his wife in a nonjudgmental manner, or being noncritical about what she is saying; but if he does not try to actually identify with her, and with what she is trying to say, the conversation is stifled.

A young wife recently had made a practice of talking with her husband *before* dinner, discussing with him those things she thought important and offering her thoughts to him for his consideration. But his mind never seemed to be with her.

I asked her if he liked to eat. She said he loves to, and had been skipping lunch to lose weight. His mind was on the future–what to eat and how good it was going to be. I suggested that possibly the evening conversation be after dinner. It worked. He just hadn't been with her mentally. His mind was ahead of hers. Once his hunger pangs were quieted, he was with her.

To get the maximum enjoyment out of talking to each other, each partner must be aware of the mental, as well as the physical and psychological, presence of the other.

There are many additional things married people can do to come closer when they are talking to each other. One of them is to avoid talking things over when either partner is antagonistic or upset. Being upset is just not conducive to *rational*, let alone enjoyable, discussion. In this case it is best to separate physically for awhile until the upset partner is calm enough to discuss things. Don't make the mistake of discussing what you were upset about as you come back together.

When you come together after a disagreement, reestablish some common rapport, and find some simple, interesting things you can talk about. Talk about something that both of you enjoy. Make it difficult for you to disagree on the subject.

Don't go over the past. Don't rehash or recall things that will only stir painful memories. This will immediately drive a wedge between you.

If money is a big problem, one of the worst things a couple can do after a disagreement is to begin talking about money. They are simply beginning on the worst of possible terms with a topic proven to be sensitive to both of them. The relationship is still too weak and fragile to subject it to something which it is not ready to handle. Begin first by each asking the other what he or she did that day. Work at building a rational and caring exchange.

Pete and Linda followed this idea. Money problems were the biggest concern in their marriage. They often had spats over each other's spending habits and their financial condition in general. After some counseling, they learned to separate when they became upset with each other. *They talked things over when both of them were calm.* They began by talking about anything pleasant they had done during the day. *They knew money problems were to be brought up after both were calm and after they had reestablished good feelings between them.*

When Pete and Linda got back together and began talking, Pete did the right thing by asking what Linda had done that afternoon. She told him about what she had done around the house. From this conversation, Pete ignored the fact that she had spent most of her time with their two preschool children, and instead made a comment about the possibility of her buying something she didn't need from a telephone solicitor or a door-to-door salesman. Bingo! They were right back into an argument about money. Pete had violated the second rule of the "presence" theory by prejudging Linda. He had not waited to think about what she had said. Although he was in her "physical" and "mental" presence, he certainly was not in her "psychological" presence. He had critically prejudged her and that turned off Linda's talking to him. The talk had rapidly turned from something pleasant to a resumption of their disagreement over money.

Anything that "puts down" another person is a real inhibitor to effective communication. Two people just cannot talk to each other and enjoy it if one person is judging the other by criticizing or belittling. Even when value judgments are being made, it is imperative these be made carefully from a calm emotional condition.

It is also important that the judgments be rendered only when the relationship has gained strength. Listen thoughtfully to your partner and then express your own thoughts on the subject, and allow time for both opinions without cutting or hurting the other. The use of language like "You're dumb" or "That's the stupidest thing you've ever said" is certainly not conducive to building a relationship. Statements like "You're weird, you're really weird" certainly cast doubt upon the self-image and self-worth of a person. Such statements undermine the possibility of a closer relationship.

Belittling, putting someone down verbally, and ridiculing all mean the same thing. They are verbal communications that subject the other person to degradation. When we discussed immobilizing people by not allowing for alternatives, we learned what happens when a person finds *himself* being personally criticized rather than criticizing what he *says*. The courses of action left open in such a situation are greatly reduced. The person's defense mechanisms come into play and barriers form. These barriers inhibit conversation and remove the joy of sharing.

Jean and Fred were a good example of what I am trying to say. When they were first married, they used to spend hours together talking about all kinds of things. One day Jean mentioned something about her boss at work. Fred was highly critical of her for being upset with her employer, so Jean stopped talking about her boss. Then Fred mentioned a cute, sexy secretary with a short skirt, and Jean got upset. So Fred avoided not only talking about this secretary but any other cute, sexy girls he saw. Another time, Jean was complaining about her mother, and Fred became critical. What Fred and Jean were doing was following the rule: any time you find difficulty talking with your partner about something, you avoid it. Their fear was that every time they opened their mouths they would be criticized, and so they thought it better not to talk. As the months went on, they began to talk less and less. Then they came to see me and said they had a problem in their marriage—no communication. They had a lot to talk about, but they hadn't learned to talk or listen with kindness and courtesy.

Just talking things over is no solution to problems when the conversation is likely to cause pain. Desire or motivation is not a sufficient answer to problem-solving. A couple may have all the necessary desire to get along, but they must learn certain practical rules that underlie compatibility. Even if two people are close to each other, bad habits, like lecturing, judging, and nagging, all hinder them from a growing and deepening relationship.

We have been exploring sound principles of how people can talk to each other and get the most out of it. There are still those who will say, "We do all these things; but we still don't enjoy talking to each other. We don't argue or belittle each other. We respect each other. We listen to each other, but we just don't have much to say to each other anymore." In this event, we must look at what such couples are actually doing with their lives.

Lou and June, both in their middle fifties, had just moved into a townhouse. When they were young and dating, they had been very happy together. They talked with each other incessantly. Through the early years of marriage they had a stable relationship. They had children, like most couples, and did all the things that most of us do in the early years of marriage. Over the years they grew apart gradually, almost without noticing.

After their children were married, Lou and June had sold their home and moved into a new townhouse complex nearby. It was then that they began to notice that things were awfully quiet. They didn't have a lot to say to each other anymore. What had gone wrong?

They still said that they loved each other, but somewhere in the complexity of their marital relationship these two people felt things were no longer the same. The signals being sent by their nervous systems to their brains were telling them that something was wrong in their marriage.

Lou and June seldom had any disagreements. They just weren't able to talk to each other and find conversation enjoyable. June said talking to Lou had become like talking to a wall. Although they talked about the "little things," as all couples do, they did not find many things of mutual interest. They weren't living in complete silence, but as June said, "It was simply work to talk to each other."

Their problem was one familiar to many couples after the children have gone. Later in the book I will discuss how children add a tremendous amount of depth to a marriage.

Depth is the amount of involvement we have with one another, the things we have in common, things two people share. When a couple is dating and enjoying such a variety of things as going to plays, eating out, traveling or playing at various sports, these activities form a basis which helps to provide depth in a relationship. When children come into a relationship, many couples build the depth of their relationship around the children. If the kids are in Little League, the mother will become involved in the pop concession to help raise money for uniforms. Dad will be umpiring or coaching the team, helping in some way. Mom and dad go to the games and find other couples with similar interests. So new friendships are formed. Mother washes the little hero's uniform when he comes home and dad talks to him about how things went during the game. All this is providing depth to the marriage.

A daughter might come home and ask dad to help with a science project. The father might saw the lumber and wire a few electrical devices for a science project while the mother might see that the end product is tasteful and attractive. Depth, in this case, is built around children.

As children grow older, and one becomes involved in the school play, the bands, athletics and the like, more and more depth in a marriage continues to revolve around the children. It is easy and natural for this to happen. Parents are happy when their children are interested and involved in many activities. In turn, the parents get involved as a result of the children's interests.

If the children like swimming, the family becomes involved with activities centered around swimming. Just transporting children to their various activities can be time-consuming. Often the children learn to like some activities simply because the parents are already enthusiastic about them. So children learn involvement from the parents. Most of the depth and the conversation in any home centers around such activities and interests. Therein lies a problem yet to come.

If a couple builds the depth of their adult interpersonal relationship largely on what the children are doing, later in the marriage it will be necessary to develop other common interests to continue depth in the marriage. Children leaving invariably results in a partial vacuum. Love must be reinforced every day of the marriage, and especially at this time. When the children are gone, mom and dad again seem to be like a young couple going out on dates. This seems to be ideal. Mom and dad are really enjoying each other and life with no one else to look out for and less strain on the budget. But for the couple which does not build the depth into their relationship, or is not aware they must continually build upon the depth already there, the marriage will begin to die.

Communication in marriage is based on two people talking with each other about their common interests. The key to relaxed, pleasant talking is finding a basis for a relationship between two people so that they really have a lot in common to talk about. Talking is simply a pleasurable and enjoyable part of human relationships. Where a relationship lacks depth, especially in the post-children family, there is very little indeed to talk about. And the silence can be deafening.

After their children were grown, Lou and June suffered from a lack of depth in their relationship. June was a supervisor at a commercial laundry, and Lou was a construction foreman. They sat around the apartment in the evening watching TV, then went to bed. Lou and June had very little in common that they wanted to share. Love and depth in any relationship require constant attention. Couples who enjoy being together have things in common, like similar interests and hobbies. Couples who do not have much in common have trouble.

Lou and June tried to build depth back into their marriage. They started by taking turns at planning the weekends. June wanted to go to a local art gallery and then out to dinner to be followed later in the evening by taking in a new movie. This activity gave them a lot to talk about for several days. In addition to doing something together, they could share their reactions to the pictures, sculptures, and various works of art. They could talk about the restaurant, their favorite foods, and where they might want to go next. There was also the movie to discuss. Such possibilities multiply themselves.

On the next weekend Lou planned the activities. They went on one of those weekend package plans offered at an inn several hours from their home. The resort had a social director on weekends. There were so many things to do that even those without much imagination could stay busy. Resorts can be depth-builders. Lou and June thoroughly enjoyed their experience. They met other couples whose companionship they enjoyed. They invited several of their new acquaintances to visit at their home the next weekend.

It was not long before Lou and June had built depth back into their marriage. They were committed to making their relationship work. June summed things up one day when she said they had spent too many years together to see it all end in a divorce. So they put their minds and hearts together and again made the relationship into something beautiful and alive.

After a while, Lou and June stopped planning surprise activities. They simply enjoyed talking and planning together some things they might do on the forthcoming weekend. Again more depth was added. In retrospect, Lou and June didn't need help in learning how to talk to each other. What they needed was to relearn how to find things in common.

As I stated earlier, with some couples the keys to enjoyable conversation are physical presence, psychological presence, and openness. It is important not to prejudge your partner. When differences occur, keep the door open. The ability to develop alternatives that permit various courses of action is vital to successful marriage. Alternatives give more mobility and freedom of choice. The more choices there are, the more chances we have to find happiness.

The way in which we talk with each other can broaden or limit these choices. The type of conversation that encourages creative expression and thoughtful interaction is helped by the open-ended, opinion type of question. Such a question may have many answers, any of which may be correct.

When someone asks an open-ended question, he is not looking for a definite answer. The question itself encourages opinion and challenges the imagination. The way the question is asked provides freedom to the respondent.

Here are some examples of open-ended, thinking questions:

> If you were President, what would you do about food prices?
>
> What do you think it would be like to spend two months marooned on a tropical island with your family? With your best friend? With someone you had a difficult time getting along with?
>
> If you had $1 million and were allowed to spend $1000 a day, how would you spend it?

The idea is to allow the other person to talk, and to present his views and thoughts, without limiting him by the way the question is asked. In this process both the listener and the speaker get to know each other. This type of question increases conversation. Try it at your next party or at the dinner table this evening. First learn to identify an open-ended question. Then practice phrasing such questions.

The type of question that limits dialogue and effectively stops conversation is called a closed question. A person asking, "When did you move to Indiana?" is probably going to get some one- or two-word response like, "Oh, about 1973." Then the conversation may lag because many avenues are automatically closed. A similar open-ended question would be, "Tell me about your experience in the move to Indiana."

Good conversationalists seldom ask closed-type questions; instead they direct open-ended inquiries that draw out the other person. This then gives the impression that the inquirer is very thoughtful, interested, and pleasing to talk to. Actually, good conversationalists, like the MCs on talk shows, utilize two skills exceptionally well: They thoughtfully listen and interact with others; and they ask questions that keep the conversation going. Anyone who cares enough to make an effort at this technique can easily improve his ability to talk things over with other people.

Finally, the very act of talking brings forth the art of conversation. Conversation often gets its start, as well as being pushed along, by questions. Thus, the type of questions that are asked are important.

A question that demands just one answer does little to get things going. Questions which allow for many answers and opinions open conversation and allow for much discussion.

Also, questions which lead to creative, imaginative and thought-provoking responses create an interesting time. People enjoy thinking-type questions which evoke interest and stimulation. In this type of question, the answer is not readily apparent, but needs to be thought out.

For example, for a couple that has just been to a movie, a question might be, "Could you think of anyone that might be added to the story but not change the story?" Another might involve three different endings that would have made the movie more enjoyable.

But regardless how you do it, it is important to learn the art of conversation. Talking is what we humans do most when we are together; and if we want to stay together, we should be constantly working on the art of conversation.

Chapter eleven

Differences in men and women

Much has been written about the psychological makeup of men and women. Some emphasize differences and others stress similarities between the sexes. Still other writings state that each human being has differences which make that person so complex psychologically that one cannot generalize about the differences in men and women.

I believe that the two sexes generally look at life in a somewhat different manner. Besides the obvious physiological distinctions, I believe there are also differences in the way men and women generally think about things. Obviously we notice differences in people that constitute their individual psychological makeup. But in addition to these differences I believe that there are some general differences. How many of these differences may actually be culturally learned effects, rather than innate qualities, I do not know. Perhaps it is not so important to know *why* men and women view things differently. It is important to know *that* there are some differences.

In this chapter we will explore these differences and show how they come into focus in a marital relationship. The comments and observations I will make about how men and women think are largely based on human nature as I see it now in the mid-1970s.

It is obvious that there has been a major change during the past generation in how women think. Prior to the late 1940s or early 1950s, the major concern of a typical woman in relationship to her mate revolved around security and survival. Security–in that a woman looked to her man for support, food, clothing, and shelter. A woman expected that her basic needs would be met and her survival assured. A woman who looked for romance in her man above and beyond all material concerns often lived to regret her oversight. Many stories have been written about women who sacrificed everything for the men they loved, but their sacrifices led only to tragedy because the men couldn't provide for them. Most women were foresighted enough to consider the practical qualities of a potential mate. Romance was always important, but years ago there was more emphasis on survival and security.

A change in the thinking patterns of women began about 1950. World War II interrupted the psychological effects of the post-Depression period of two generations ago and hastened this change. The post-Depression period and the post-World War II period both contributed to the economic well-being of most people in the United States.

Many of us have heard and read about the terrible days of the Great Depression in the 1920s and 1930s. In fact, the psychological effects of the Depression were far worse than the economic effects. Today we have welfare, relief, social security, and many other benefits, all of which can be largely attributed to the psychological effects of the Depression. These systems added security and opened up opportunities for women. The dependency of women upon men for security and survival began to diminish.

I have read about cultures of centuries ago where women and sometimes men were turned out to die in the elements after a certain age. In those cultures, woman's dependency upon man for survival and security was maximal. In modern societies women are no longer dependent upon man for everything. In fact, it has become incumbent upon American men to see that their women are cared for either through insurance or through the woman's ability to earn a living should something happen to him. Millions of American women have been encouraged by their husbands to have assurances of security by holding their teaching certificates or through a nursing certificate or some kind of business acumen. The idea is the same: Security is assured. The result is that women are not really as dependent on men as they once were.

Divorce rates were astoundingly low years ago, perhaps for a multitude of reasons. One factor was noticeable then: A woman had little opportunity to earn a living. In other words, there was little security for her should she be divorced or deserted by her husband. This factor, in itself, can be attributed to holding down divorce rates, and it undoubtedly had an effect on the morality of the time.

Today, modern woman looks at life in an entirely different manner. Now she looks for a man with whom she can live and actually share her life. She is looking for a companion, a friend, as well as a lover and father of her children. A woman is looking for someone in whom she can believe, and with whom she can relate her experiences. The cultural changes in living have also brought about changes in what women want out of marriage and how they perceive marital life.

Women have always sought a sincere, authentic type of loving relationship with their husbands. Prior to recent times, few women thought they could actually hold out to get that. They often took the first offer of marriage and did not hold out for "true love." Parents were anxious to see their daughter marry, for then the parents felt assured of the daughter's security and that the daughter's needs for future survival would be met. A woman had someone to take care of her. Now, women see happiness and involvement in a marriage as their greatest need. It can be illustrated in this fashion:

Before the 1950s

⇒ Marriage ⇒ *External needs* dominate thinking and marital relationships: "getting a husband," security, food, clothing, shelter, children, home.

After the 1950s

⇒ Marriage ⇒ *Internal needs* dominate relationships: authentic love, common interests, happiness, worthwhile activities and career.

Since there has been a change in the way women think, the man who comes home and says he "brought home the paycheck—what else can his wife want?" is in for trouble. To have successful marital relationships today, men must be more willing to work at a marriage by sharing themselves intellectually and psychologically, and by doing things that both he and his wife enjoy.

Women are more person-oriented than men. Women associate what they are doing with whom they are doing it. To a woman, the person with whom she is doing something is often more important than what she is doing. Most women will tell you it is not really their love for bowling that causes them to join a bowling league; rather, it is the friends and companionship they enjoy. The primary reason most women join a club or organization is the sociability; the second reason is the activity itself. Mothers have traditionally carried most of the responsibility for the socializing process of their children. Men, on the other hand, will enjoy bowling mostly for bowling's sake. It is the activity itself that is more important to a man than a woman. Men are very sensitive about their scores. A man is more "thing" or "activity" oriented. A man can tinker with motors or inanimate objects for hours. A woman looks at him and can't understand what a man sees in something that doesn't talk back and contribute to social interaction. A woman I know once told me she loves to knit and do needlepoint, but only when she is watching a show on TV or talking with friends.

This psychological difference between men and women can be readily seen in the area of sports. Let's say two couples go to play tennis. The women usually enjoy the friendship of the other couple and like being with their husbands, while the men are often prone to become engrossed in the game itself and get competitive. A man enjoys the game because of the game itself and because of the competition, while most women enjoy the game because of the people they are sharing it with.

In addition to being more sociable, women are more affectionate or romantic than men. The fact women are this way leads some people to consider women to be the warmer and more loving sex. Although individual differences are found in all people, these are references and generalizations that apply to men and women as we analyze their behavior in marriage. When a man telephones his wife and says he is bringing home a friend for dinner, his wife is upset because she cares about the preparation that is necessary to entertain well. The husband is less concerned with details and easily overlooks how proud and sensitive a woman is about her home and social life.

Sometimes this process seems to be reversed when it comes to making certain decisions. Men like to take a lot of time reasoning to reach a conclusion. Sometimes women think it is hard to get their husbands to move. Women are inclined to make decisions more rapidly. Some refer to women's intuitive power. When the woman suddenly says to her husband that she has just decided that . . . , his response is usually that he believes they should go more slowly, think about it for awhile, or wait and see. On occasion, when a husband asks his wife how she arrived at a decision, his wife may say, "I don't know; I just did." Those are happy couples who learn to find alternative courses of action that permit both parties to be happy—so that together they can be one and yet each can be himself.

Generally, men are less sensitive than women. They tend to poke fun at each other, sometimes with biting remarks—all in fun, perhaps, and usually taken that way. But a husband should be a little cautious if he is tempted to treat his wife as "one of the boys." Normally her sensitivity will incline her to respond poorly to such kidding.

Most women are very sensitive when it comes to being teased, especially about their bodies. Yet many husbands love to tease on just that subject. They are less likely to kid about other things, like her ability to ski. Even then, most women find it hard to endure the kidding men are accustomed to. Sooner or later, a wife will get irritated with a tease. I have a good friend who has called me "Skinny" (and I call him "Fatty") for many years. His wife still continues to try to smooth things over whenever we talk like this. I have never heard a woman call another woman "fatty" or "skinny." It would be far too personal for them. Couples are well-advised to be aware of this important difference between man and woman.

Men are proud. A man likes to think he is great as a person. It is as dangerous for a woman to step on her husband's pride as it is for a husband to tease about his wife's appearance.

Because man has been the stronger physically, women have learned to get along with man by not challenging him. This is most noticeable in the way women talk to men. When a woman says to her husband, "Are you going downtown?" she is asking for a ride to town. What the wife is really saying is, "Will you take me downtown?" but women are frequently not as direct as their husbands. Men are usually more direct. They are blunt (sometimes too blunt) and come directly to the point.

Since many women tend to express themselves indirectly, a husband is well-advised to listen for what his wife means as well as to what she says. In most cases women should learn to accept what their husbands say for what it is and not read in an indirect meaning that was never there.

Perhaps in carving out a living, man has learned to be more calculating; while women, by virtue of their historical role, have learned to be more indirect and tactful. If a husband's response to the question "Are you going downtown?" is "No," then he has not heard the real question. He would do better to respond with "Do you want to go along?" or "Can I get you something?" These answers lead the way to constructive discussion and reinforce the woman's position in the marriage relationship.

Men and women tend to adapt to their roles as fathers and mothers differently. Women are obviously more committed to their role by their very nature. Their role is very real to them. Men have to learn what it is to be fathers. They have to work at it. Although some women have to develop an understanding of their role as mother, almost all men have to work at learning how to fill their responsibility. It is important for a woman to understand how her husband will probably have to adapt to this new situation. To some extent and where necessary men, too, might be able to help their wives to an understanding of motherhood, but for the most part women adapt far more easily.

The following differences are all generalities and there are many exceptions to them. Also, change is swift at this point in history. Nevertheless, I maintain that these generalizations are still valid and important. Most women are more religious than men. Women are more intuitive and sensitive. Men tend to be more skeptical. Generally men ask more questions and are harder to convince. Many women are altruistic and unsuspecting. A woman has more faith. A woman is more optimistic. A woman is more easily encouraged by what she sees and is more easily consoled. A man is pessimistic and more easily discouraged. The adage that behind every great man is a great woman recognizes that women are especially adept at providing inspiration, the optimism, and the unrelenting faith that everything will work out.

Today some women seek their own place in the sun. Men especially (obviously women, too) look for recognition and success. People have a very strong drive for prestige and status. In fact, many men have a greater drive for recognition than for sex. A man wants, needs, and strives to be somebody important. Some men seem to have an incurable ambition. Men have two focal centers: 1) their marriage, children, family; and 2) jobs or careers. In contrast, most women have *traditionally* had only one focal center—marriage, children, family. This, too, is changing as the role of modern woman is changing.

Men have been taught to mask many of their emotions. They are told at an early age that little boys don't cry and they are encouraged to be big and strong like daddy. Women are less ashamed of emotions. The saying "Isn't that like a woman?" or "She's just like her mother" gives the young girl an outlet for emotions that basically say society accepts demonstrative feelings from the female sex. The future may bring change in this area, also, as men become more conscious of their masks. But we speak in the present.

I have purposefully stayed away from mentioning the psychological differences in how men and women perceive sex because it is discussed in the chapter on love and sex. But a mention of the basic differences is in order here. The important difference is that women look at sex and associate the sex act with a person. The person with whom they are having sex is more important than just the physical pleasure they receive from actual intercourse.

Most men perceive the sex act differently. They too seek the sensual physical pleasure derived from sex. As a rule men do not strongly associate sex with the person, at least not to the extent that women do. Men often look at a woman in terms of the physical pleasure they can receive from her body. This is often disgusting to a woman whose psychological outlook is usually very different. To most women, man is some sort of "animal" when he behaves in a way that lacks respect for their person. Women see sex as an expression of love. Women see sex as an outgrowth of an authentic human relationship of involvement in which the two care deeply for each other. The woman is saying she loves someone and hopes that someone loves her; but men are more motivated toward the physical, sensual pleasures. Men can be promiscuous; women tend to be loyal.

Women have a more total outlook on life; that is, women usually see the whole spectrum of things. Most men tend to compartmentalize and sequence things. Some people interpret this as part of man's practical nature. But since many men do not look at things wholly, they do think quite often of sex as compartmentalized–a separate part of life. Women view the sex act only in relationship to the involvement, and thus associate sex and person together.

There are other psychological differences I have not referred to in this chapter, because I have tried to emphasize the differences most essential to an understanding of how to make a marriage successful. What we have discussed here also applies to common needs of all people in any male-female relationship. Although men and women do have some distinct differences, ultimately all people have similar basic needs for acceptance and love and the desire to lead a happy life.

Chapter twelve

Looking at what people do

In today's society more than in any other period of history, men and women need to develop strong identities. These will be based upon our ability to discover rewarding, involving relationships with others. It is in these relationships that we can find success experiences. Although some may find reward and accomplishment on an individual basis, no one ever accomplishes anything totally on his own. In marriage, more than in any other human endeavor, the success is dependent upon the effort of two people. There is little room for assumption about what the other person believes or is thinking. It is important to know; it is dangerous to assume. Later in married life many begin to assume what their partner believes and what he or she thinks. These people will never know for certain what their partners think, but they claim they have been living together for so long they know their partner in every way possible.

If you are of this opinion, it is quite simple to test your belief. Ask yourself these questions: What is his or her favorite food? Favorite color? What does he or she like to do best? What would he or she most like to do? What about retirement plans? Travel plans? Write down your answers. Then ask your partner to check them and see how accurate your assumptions were. These were easy questions. Consequently, many of you may have done well. Here are questions to test your assumptions a little further:

What are the things I do that he or she enjoys?

What are his or her happiest moments?

What things would he or she really love to do?

When did he or she last enjoy himself or herself?

What is most important to him or her?

What does he or she think about the most?

Jot down your answers on a piece of paper and see how much you are assuming about your marital relationship. The point I want to emphasize is that assumptions in any relationship can become a barrier to growth. If the assumptions are incorrect, they can cause the two people to move apart. It is easy to look at each other's behavior over the years and make quick assumptions.

On Sunday afternoons, when one football game follows the other on TV with irresistible urgency, a wife might experience what I refer to as "snowball thoughts." This is a form of assuming. Things start out like, "He's watching the game again. Well, he has worked hard all week. That's OK. One game." But soon he is watching games for hours on end, especially on those holiday weekends when it is possible to actually lose yourself in the TV tube. To a woman who is person-oriented and wants involvement, this is very frustrating. She would like to talk, to do something. He may be tired and he likes sports and so will find no difficulty in becoming totally absorbed in watching unending athletic games on TV. The disagreement arises not only because of the psychological differences in men and women, but because quite often she interprets her husband's preoccupation with sports and TV as neglect of her. As snowballing begins, she develops doubts and fears about their relationship. As the snowball rolls and picks up speed, it gathers all the hurts and grievances of a decade into one fast-growing missile about to explode.

As I stated earlier, assumptions in marriage relationships can be deadly. If a wife says, "He loves those football games more than he loves me. He never did really love me," she is making an assumption. I have tried to convince such football widows that this seeming neglect is not necessarily a loss of love, and that such a conclusion is a dangerous assumption. I expect a retort like "He likes the TV more than he likes me." Now that's a large assumption.

Here is another example. A woman might have had a man who called her a half dozen times a day. Then suddenly he only calls her once or twice a week. She concludes, "He doesn't love me as much anymore." Or consider the husband whose wife called him at work every day at ten o'clock. Several days last week she didn't call him. Now he begins thinking, "Well, I'm not going to call her." He wonders what has happened in their relationship. He might go home that evening and ask her what's wrong. If he's really worked up, he may enter with "What the hell is wrong with you? How come you don't call me anymore?" It doesn't take much to see how two people involved in snowball thinking can move apart in their marital relationship.

The person snowballing in his thought process is behaving rashly. His thought patterns are illustrated in the following pattern:

1st	2nd	3rd	4th
Looking ⟶	Assuming ⟶	Prejudging ⟶	Reacting

Making assumptions is one of the hazards to a growing relationship. When people are dating, they seldom make a lot of assumptions about each other because they do not know each other well enough. Once married we begin to make all kinds of assumptions about our partners.

Closely associated with assumptions is labeling. By this I mean a person looks at another, makes a judgment about him or her (which may or may not be true) and with this label allows that judgment to affect his activity with that person. Labeling a person has three effects: 1) it prevents a person from seeing another in anything but the assigned role, 2) it immobilizes a person in terms of moving toward another in any sort of relational way, and 3) it makes a person relate toward others according to their labeled expectations.

For example, if a man labels his wife as a bad cook, he is surprised when she puts a good meal on the table. Then he reminds her and others of the bad meals he usually has at home. Also, to follow this example through, it would be hard for him to develop any kind of loving relationship at mealtime if he is constantly reminding his wife of her failures. And finally his wife, who picks up this failure view of her cooking from her husband, begins to believe it and to behave as a bad cook. Frankly, if both are working, he should try cooking. Many men, for one reason or another, have begun to learn and enjoy creative cooking.

Partners should look for the successes in each other's lives and think about them. This leads to another consideration. As people make it up the occupational ladder to success, they often *assume* their relationship with their partner is equally successful. While working at their job, they quit working at the relationship and assume it will always be there. This is foolish. Often the price of succeeding at the office is made at the expense of the marriage. Also, the direction in which the success leads may not be to the best interest of the marriage. Success comes from achievement in careers, clubs, from higher salaries, and so on. While a healthy family life may have contributed to a person's success, it is nevertheless true that the success itself is often not within the marital relationship but in something external to the marriage itself. The opportunities for finding success outside the marriage are more numerous than ever before for both men and women. The following illustration exemplifies these opportunities:

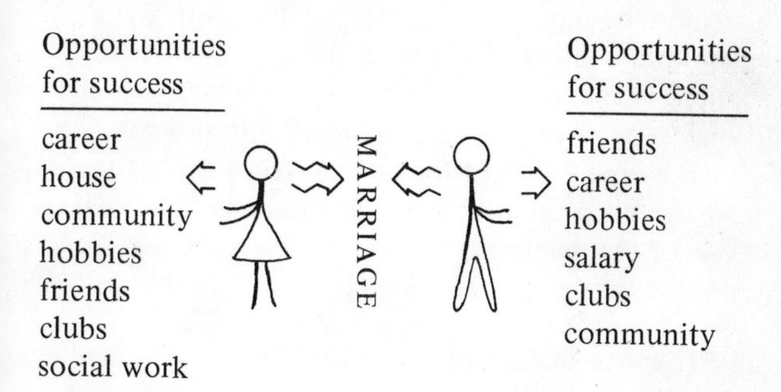

To have a successful marriage, efforts must be made to maintain a cohesiveness, a togetherness, toward each partner. The marriage, to be a rewarding one, must encompass the combined efforts of two people.

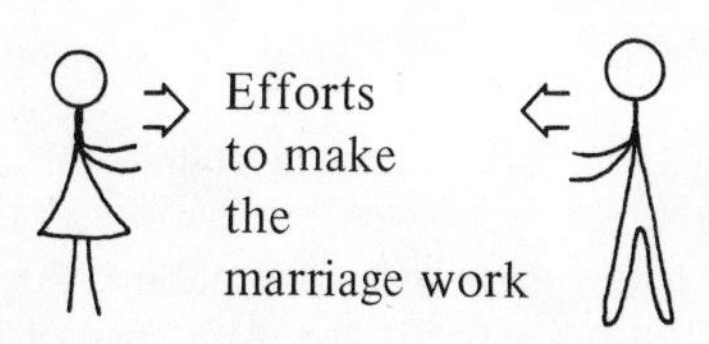

Of course, the degree to which any marriage ultimately succeeds or fails is whether or not the basic needs of the two people involved are met.

When two people decide they love each other and are willing to make lasting commitments to each other, they get married. They begin sharing more and moving closer together throughout their lives. The common interests they have build a depth and add to the loving relationship between the two people.

Assumptions and labeling are often reckless and cause hardships in any relationship. To find success in their marriage together, they must both work at their relationship, and they must not label or assume things about each other.

Another important aspect of "looking at what people do" in marriage is to look at the effort the couple is making. The first is the couple's conscientious effort at making their relationship work. The second aspect is that their efforts are made constantly, and the third point is that they make these efforts in a consistent manner.

Visualize them in this way:

Efforts to make a marriage work
need to be made:

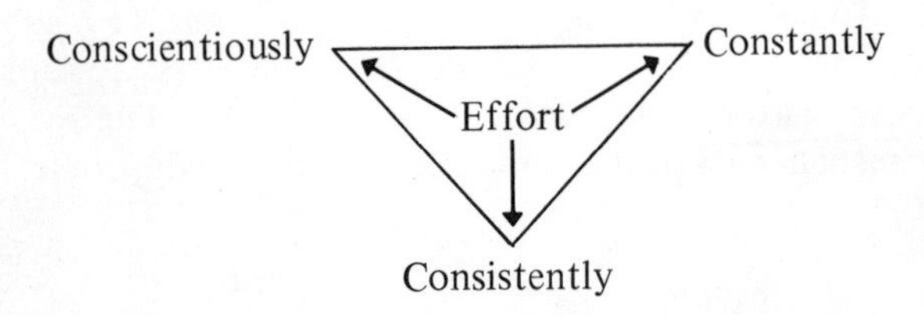

People ask me, "How can I make my marriage work?" I believe the answer begins in the degree of commitment each partner has to making the relationship work. Commitment is essential because out of commitment comes your basic desire and motivation to make the marriage work. The desire and motivation then enable you to make your efforts more conscientiously, constantly, and consistently.

One young fellow sitting in my office one night said, "I should have loved her more." He was feeling depressed. His wife had left him a month earlier. In reflecting back over his words, what he was saying was that his efforts at making the marriage work should have been more consistent, conscientious, and constant. After they had been married a short time, he began to take his wife for granted. He quit working at the relationship. The zing between them rapidly disappeared.

You have to work at any relationship. The happiness you receive from marriage is in direct proportion to the energies you put forth to make the thing work. Someone once said:

Happiness equals Reality minus Expectations

Reality in life is to view the world as it is. We all have reasonable control over the reality of our lives, but we have a great deal of control over our expectations. When reality succeeds or surpasses our expectations, especially in marriage, we're OK. We are happy and satisfied. When our expectations surpass what we receive in reality, then we become dissatisfied. This is the way it is in marriage when the fantasies we bring into a relationship do not materialize.

Some couples who are apart for a long time begin to fantasize about the relationship they had. Memories are funny things. We all like to remember the good times, but time also distorts reality. If a couple's memories lead them to expectations that exceed the realities of their relationship, when they get back together they're going to be in for trouble.

The answer for them is in the amount of effort that both partners make that enables them to come closer together. What these efforts do is to bring our expectations closer into harmony with reality. We have to work at being happy.

I also believe that making a marriage work today is tougher than ever before. People have come to expect more out of life. They are no longer satisfied with many aspects of life that had satisfied their parents and grandparents. Our expectations today are far more refined. A woman who once might have been satisfied to sit at home and take care of the kids, while her husband went fishing or hunting with his buddies, will no longer put up with this. What once she was willing to accept without question, she now sees as important–namely the ongoing relationship itself. Accordingly, people now expect more from marriage. We should remember that not every competent person automatically gets along well with every other competent person. If two people want to get along, they simply can't assume a lot about the other person, and they also have to conscientiously, consistently, and constantly put forth efforts at getting along.

Marriage works best when people put effort into it. It's like putting gas into a car to get it to run, or like rowing a boat to get where you want to be. Each has to be constantly refueled, checked, and worked at. The good feelings we get in marriage are returns on the investments from doing things together that we enjoy. The closer the relationship, the more the two partners have worked at it . . . they have done a lot of things to make each other feel this way. Efforts and work keep a relationship moving. If a couple is blasé about their marriage, that's the way it is . . . blasé. Their marriage will be blah without some effort.

We must also remember marriage has many faces. The idea of intimacy can be easily misunderstood. In addition to the efforts toward each other, people sometimes need a little breathing space from each other. Psychic distance between two people is also a necessary part of a loving relationship. Every one of us at one time or another needs time to reflect, to meditate, to be alone. Taking a long, leisurely walk outdoors alone or curling up in our favorite chair with a good book once in a while gives us psychic space to do some reflective thinking. The physical and psychological togetherness in marriage is good, but we also have to remember that occasionally we need some time to ourselves. Such time can later serve to strengthen the marriage, making your life together much more enjoyable and fun.

Privacy is a precious gift to anyone. The reason for marriage is not to smother the other person completely by a togetherness that overwhelms him or her. I find some people are much more receptive and helpful to each other after they have had some "catching up" time.

As human beings we all have interests that bring us enjoyment and into the company of others. We associate with people who like to do the same things. This makes us happy and gives us a sense of fulfillment. We share our joy with others we care about. In marriage, partners cannot always be expected to be tuned into the same things at the same time, so the natural thing to do is to allow each other some room or freedom.

The idea of respecting the other's need for some occasional psychic privacy gives both partners a feeling of mutual respect, and strengthens the bond between them. It allows the relationship to grow and spiral upward.

Chapter thirteen

TV: diversion or obsession?

Census data indicates that 96% of the homes in America have one or more television sets. The average home set is on more than six hours daily. For most Americans, television viewing is a daily experience. The average number of viewing hours for adults is about 4½ hours per day. Most children are avid TV viewers, and some studies conclude that children watch TV an average of six to seven hours daily. One study revealed that preschool children watch TV as much as eight hours a day. It is said that by the time children reach their teens, they will have spent more time in front of TV than they have spent in school.

The U.S. Department of Health, Education and Welfare has issued a report entitled Television and Growing Up: The Impact of Televised Violence by the Surgeon General's Scientific Advisory Committee on Television and Social Behavior. The report was published in 1972 and presented some interesting findings relative to the amount of television we watch. For instance, this study discloses that most people watch TV at least four hours daily. Frequent TV viewing begins about the age of three and remains relatively high until the age of twelve when viewing begins to decline. When young people marry and have families, their TV viewing time tends to rapidly increase, and then remains stable through their middle adult years. After middle age, when the children leave home, the amount of TV watching increases even further.

Lyle and Hoffman, in a 1971 study reported by Murray et al., entitled Television and Social Behavior, Television's Effects: Further Explorations, say that there was a trend among first grade children who spent large amounts of time watching TV to report the lowest levels of loneliness while yet reporting the lowest frequency of play with others after school. TV is a passive instrument that by its nature does not foster creativity and social interaction. The study goes on to suggest that children with social problems turn to television to find companionship.

Another study by Murray found in the same edition as Lyle's article concludes that extremely heavy TV viewers are most likely to have problems of social maladjustment: to be passive in interpersonal situations, to be bashful, to be more distractable. Murray suggests that heavy TV viewing is a symptom, not a cause of the individual's retreat from social interaction.

Regardless of whether or not TV is a cause or a symptom, the point is that excessive TV watching does not foster, encourage, or help one to develop the ability to socially interact with others. Television creates an illusion of involvement for the viewer—an illusion that he is involved with others, that everything is all right. Television offers emotional stimulation without the risk of actual involvement. A housewife who watches a soap opera becomes involved emotionally, temporarily, and vicariously with the heartaches of the moment. But she can turn off the melodrama and not actually feel the pain of what the actors would be going through in real-life situations. Reality becomes distorted. An artificial world has been created in which people kill, rob, or achieve millions of dollars while not actually feeling the realities of life. The distinction between the real and the artificial becomes blurred. The viewer sees a world on TV and, after awhile, feels that this is *the* world.

By nightly immersion in TV, the viewer identifies with the "awesomeness" of the TV world. As he looks at his everyday affairs and responsibilities, it is easy for him to ask why he should face the drudgery of a ho-hum existence when, with no effort, he can be part of a TV fantasy world that is so much more exciting.

The illusion of TV-land can pose a serious problem for the addicted watcher. The most alarming part is that the viewer actually comes to deny it is fantasy. He actually believes that you can accept the responsibility without working at it. TV usually doesn't present a lot of shows that concern responsibility, work, and effort. Shoot-em-up, but they all walk away; slug it out, but no one gets hurt; laugh it up, but what's really so funny? The goal is distraction, to help you forget your troubles, but your troubles won't go away while you sit there.

The TV versions of some major events have come to seem more authentic than the actual occurrences themselves. TV tends to emphasize the sensational parts. This is also so because of not only the repetitive nature of TV, but because of the credibility Americans have placed in science and accordingly in the electronic eye of the TV tube. Hence the phrase "I know it's true; I saw it on TV." Instant wealth, instant fun, instant anything can be achieved by turning on the TV tube. No responsibility, no work, and no involvement. TV is primarily entertainment and fantasy. It does not provide real security. It never says you have to work hard to be productive. The motto of TV is "Everything comes out all right."

TV shows the experts, the pros, the very best. But it doesn't show the work involved in becoming that expert–the hundreds of hours of practice, the drudgery. Instead TV is turning us into a nation of spectators with no effort or work required. We just live the enjoyment vicariously. We want to be happy, and we are taught by TV that it is sinful to be unhappy.

Obviously, some television is good, relaxing, and enjoyable. But when it becomes too much a part of our life, or when it takes the place of people, especially people we love, then we had better look out.

Some viewers want to live real life in the same way they live it vicariously on television. If the TV program is boring, change the channel. We have begun to think that we must be amused or entertained while we remain passive, and that life will be full of exciting, "different," and varied stimuli that arrive upon our senses every thirty minutes. It is here that some real misfortune or heartache lies. When problems arrive in real life, the channel cannot be changed to eliminate them. The instant magic of the TV world has no counterpart in the everyday world of reality and living.

Some facets of TV culture undoubtedly have beneficial effects on our lives and marriages and, in fact, on all interpersonal relationships. Television imparts a tremendously strong message that cannot be denied. It offers high expectations, and it offers them to everyone. The advertising people have been able to convince millions of people that beer drinkers become more sociable. Thus, the implication is that by drinking beer a person automatically has more friends and is a happier person. Perfume makes us lovable. Toothpaste makes us sexy. Soap makes us nice to be with.

There are a lot of promises, unfortunately, far more than life itself has to offer. We come to believe in illusion, to forget, or worse, ignore the risk and involvement that real life requires.

In addition to living in a world of illusions, TV buffs become alienated from themselves as well as from others. With their week of watching carefully planned, the fanatic will no longer know or care what he is doing or what others around him are doing. Instead, he is immersed only in what is happening on the screen. Many families will watch TV for hours, saying nothing to each other. The majority of whatever conversation occurs is concerned with what is taking place on the screen.

Why risk a dull conversation with a friend when you can turn on any number of programs and share in the painless thrills and excitement of beautiful people. I've heard some housewives say that if it weren't for the TV, they would be "bored to tears." TV is their source of information, knowledge, news, romance, and what is worse, the main source of any emotional stimulation. It is their window to the world. A woman will alienate herself from friends and activities and sacrifice her own initiative and creativity by spending the precious, unrepeatable years of her life just "looking." Ultimately such a person becomes "conditioned" to passivity. Involvement with others becomes hard work and involves risk. How many lives that will never really be enjoyed are given up by those who lose themselves in soap operas and old movies?

The direct result of this innocuous passivity is the deterioration of interpersonal relationships. Sooner or later trouble starts. "You never take me out any more"; "I might as well be a maid"; "You never talk to me"; "I don't know what's wrong with the children; they don't seem to be interested in anything."

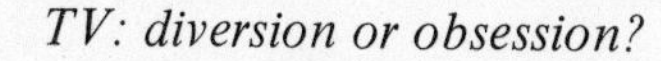

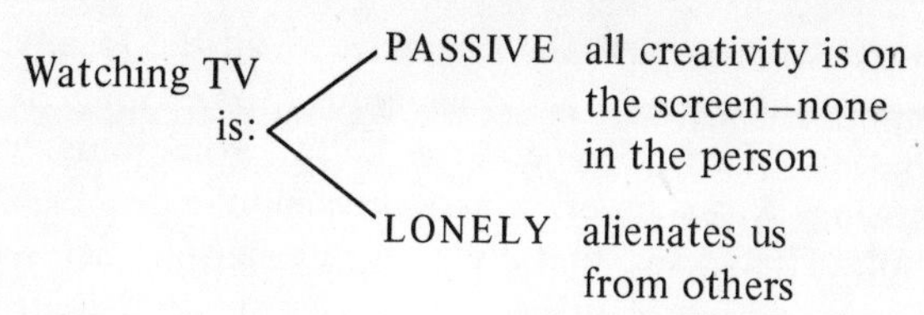

When TV becomes more important than the people around us, a progressive deterioration of interpersonal relationships will result.

TV is good when—

1 used selectively as a means for stimulating conversation
2 used in measured amounts for relaxation
3 used educationally for personal growth.

Television, according to a nationally known economist, is one of the "prime instruments for the manipulation of consumer demands." By spending excessive amounts of time watching television, the person is lured away from life and from individuality. To the unaware this preoccupation with distraction becomes an opiate, a prophylactic insulating him from reality.

One client, Judy, a young newlywed of only six months, confided to me that she watched about twelve hours of TV a day, almost every day! She got up at 7:00 A.M. to get her husband off to work and turned on the TV set while they were having breakfast. It continued to play all day as she cleaned, cooked and did her daily household tasks. She knew every program and the schedules of all the local stations. She could recite many of the commercials. Despite her involvement with TV, something was missing. A certain emptiness or vacuum led to melancholy. Judy was literally changing herself, her self-image, and her identity. We discover our own identity only as we relate to others. Judy's TV habits so insulated her from reality and interpersonal relationships that her own resourcefulness and creativity were being stifled. She looked to TV for company, and eventually she found loneliness and failure as a loving and worthwhile person. She sought action and sacrificed human interaction—the only thing in the world that would tell her who she was.

When an individual begins to retreat from life, he becomes alienated from others and starts to lose the desire to listen and talk effectively. This creates a loneliness that leads to even more television as a substitute for finding happiness among those very important people we love and are close to. This is why heavily TV-addicted housewives have a hard time maintaining interpersonal relationships with their husbands. This is why Judy came to see me.

I first got Judy away from TV by getting her into some volunteer work. The volunteer work opened up several job opportunities. I encouraged her to take the job which she thought might be most enjoyable. Then I got her to join a bowling league. As she became more active with others, doing things she enjoyed, Judy's life (and marriage) took on new meaning and happiness.

Many men are weekend TV addicts. They are devoid of all other desires except to watch one football game after another—punctuated briefly by food and calls of nature. The abandoned housewife develops an intense dislike for TV. Suppose she is not interested in football. Even suppose she is. An occasional football game is a treat. Constant football is a bore. What happens to the marriage? What is "pigskin pappy" really saying to his wife as he climbs into his football bag for the weekend?

Television encourages viewers to believe in and identify with super-heroes, celebrities, or TV personalities. Instead of developing their own self-identity, a sense of personal self-worth, and creative involvement with others, addicts identify with superstars. This transfer of identity is fine in an empty living room, but what happens in the game of real life? I often wonder if our TV heroes really use the products they endorse—as if we were mindless, incapable of making our own selections.

Doesn't TV fill in leisure time and help to pass away the time of day? Television should be used, but not abused. To relax and watch a ball game is one thing; but when the game becomes more important than those around you, that is the time to begin to take a hard look at your priorities. Which is more important—your wife or the program you are watching? I love to watch Walter Cronkite and the evening news, but I found myself literally breaking off a conversation with a child so that I could get to my program. I put the program above my children and that is irresponsible behavior.

More and more research is being done about the influence and impact of television. It is becoming apparent that *the nature or the process of watching television programs induces loneliness and passivity.* There is no doubt in my mind that television inhibits the social interaction process. When I was a youngster, the kids played together outside. Games and make-believe were an important part of our lives, but we ourselves created the games and scheduled our own lives. We also learned how to get along with each other. Young children today aren't learning these vital social skills when they sit in front of a TV set all day. The skills of listening, talking, and sharing are not being developed. The price of passivity is high.

One dating couple I knew, teenagers about sixteen, would sit in front of the TV for hours on weekends. That was their date. I asked the girl one day if she enjoyed this way of being together. She said "Yes." I asked her if they were getting to know each other, to know each other's likes and dislikes. She said "Yes." An illusion was created that everything in their relationship was OK, and yet she couldn't tell me one thing they had done together that involved planning and working together. If these two kids married, that is exactly what they would have to do to make the marriage a success: plan together and work together toward things mutually enjoyed and valued.

It is important and enjoyable to place limits on your TV viewing. This allows for proper social development and encourages selectivity in program selection. Several years ago there was a blackout in New York City. Electrical power was out for twenty-four hours. There was no TV to watch. Nine months later, the birth rate in that area increased sharply. Draw your own conclusions.

Some wives have said to me, as a marriage counselor, that their husbands have two primary interests–sex and TV (and in that order). Relationships like these are not healthy. They die easily. Many marriages have ended in divorce or are heading for serious trouble because TV has usurped the couple's time and energy. There is nothing left to share or grow on. It is as obvious as a candle going out for lack of oxygen.

Husbands and wives who are doing things together, who have hobbies and friends, who share the adventure of their own lives, are healthier, happier people. Their marital lives show it. They are not like the TV couple glued to the tube, whose interest both in each other and the rest of the world gradually diminishes, and whose adventure is entirely vicarious.

If even one partner in the marriage is a TV addict, the couple together must agree to limit the amount of TV they are viewing. Look for quality. Look for programs that help you grow. Be selective. It ultimately will affect your relationship, and both of your lives will suffer if you don't face this stark reality. As the commercial says, "You have only one life to live." Why give it away? It makes no sense to give your life to alcohol or dope. It makes no sense to eat without restriction to a point where you are ugly, inactive, and have endangered your life. It makes just as little sense to misuse television and lose your life to illusion.

Consider the amount of time you watch TV. Make a study of the amount of time your TV set is on each day, each week. Study your activities. Think about the things you do with your partner and your family during one week's time. Think about the number of friends you have and how often you see them. Reduce the amount of TV watching and work together at planning and doing things you both enjoy doing together. Get out. Get involved.

For some couples this would be almost like getting reacquainted. Those I have counseled told me they hadn't realized how far apart they had grown over the years. One couple had prided themselves on knowing "all the favorites" each thought the other had: the favorite drink, the favorite meal, the favorite color. They had learned these things about each other when they were twenty-one and newly married. Now they were forty-five and still assuming that they knew each other. What a foolish assumption! Taking the time to get reacquainted or just "staying acquainted" is a very enjoyable experience and vital for those couples who want to have a dynamic and growing relationship.

Can you be sexier, healthier, and happier without really trying? "Let me entertain you" has turned into "Let me 'disembrain' you." If you hope to actually realize some of the promises television offers, turn it off–often. Interpersonal relationships require time and effort, and it is only in this involvement that you will really find yourself and your identity. Limited TV viewing means more time to get to know each other, to be together, and to grow closer. Because you sit next to someone doesn't mean you are close to him or her. Discuss these ideas. Discuss them for a week. Discuss what you are doing. Plan several activities you enjoy, such as dancing, playing Scrabble or cards, bowling, visiting friends, or whatever you two decide together. Then discuss this subject again and try it for yet a second week. After that, evaluate what you have discussed. Has it made a difference? I think you'll see a much closer relationship developing. Try it. Real promise is found in personal risk and involvement. The fun is in doing things–not just in watching others.

Chapter fourteen

Love and sex

The difference between love and sex is actually quite simple. Sex is something people do naturally, while love is something people have to learn. Love is a process. Love cannot be defined, for if you have never experienced love, no one can describe it to you. Dictionary definitions are inadequate. Love is something that each person must learn by experience.

Sex is an act between two people. Sexuality is a natural part of a loving relationship between a man and a woman. Having sex does not have to be learned. I am sure that if you put two young people who are attracted to each other in a room by themselves they will have no trouble figuring out how to express their attraction and feelings through sex.

On the other side of the coin, love is more complex and must be learned. Love has to be established first and then maintained. Love between two people, to be enduring, *must be reinforced constantly*.

Children growing up in a home learn how to love and to form loving relationships by imitation and observation of their parents. If there is no love in the home, the children fail to learn about this type of relationship. Children first learn to give and receive love from parents who care about them. To learn how to love someone and how to sustain a warm, loving, caring relationship over a period of time with another person is a complicated process. Sex is not so complicated. The only thing sex is good for is sex! Sex does not help a couple do anything else. It does not help in playing golf, in going shopping, paying bills, raising children, or anything else. Sex only works for that one experience. Sex may bring two people closer together while they share each other, but unless they also work at their love relationship, the act of sex itself doesn't help their relationship. Sex can be as ugly as it is beautiful.

You may think that having sex will help solve the problems in your marriage. You may use sex to further your involvement and to add to your marital relationship. You may have the illusion that things will get better if you can just get together in bed. Sex certainly promises involvement, but not a deepening of the relationship. Sex is the result of a relationship rather than the cause.

Some couples, though, have little in common. They don't do many things together, have all sorts of conflicts and problems, yet they still have sexual relations with each other. The fighting between them is held in abeyance while they have sex. They both enjoy sex play, and it may be the one bright piece of happiness in an otherwise miserable marital relationship. During the sex act, and usually immediately before and shortly after, the intimacy promises to bring the couple closer together. It often does, but only physically, and for a short time. After that, and for the vast majority of time, the relationship becomes more important. Far be it from me to play down the importance of a good, healthy, satisfying sex life. Sex, no matter how small a role it plays, is natural and can be beautiful. Everyone knows what people go through in their lives to have sex and to find sexual fulfillment.

Earlier in this book I talked about the futility of trying to make another person love you. Love is the type of relationship that takes time to build and to evolve. Physical attraction may bring two people together, but to stay together and build a love relationship, they have to plan their lives as a "together" adventure. They have to work at building a depth relationship. They have to allow enough time for this to happen. Lasting, meaningful commitments between two people are not so easily developed. Some people never learn how to develop and enjoy such deep relationships. They find it easier to deal in surface relationships. To them, sex is fun while it lasts. After awhile, the speed and thrill vanish. Then to gain a thrill in having sex, they seek a new relationship. A spouse who gets sexually involved with a third person, while still married, has all sorts of emotions going. Those exuberant feelings usually don't last long. It might be nice for some if they did, but it has been my observation that people involved in these flighty experiences can't find lasting happiness anywhere. They are incapable of a real depth relationship.

In evaluating sex, let's face some facts. There are twenty-four hours in a day, seven days in a week. OK, now, that makes 168 hours a week and how much of that will be sex play? How much time is spent in actually having intercourse? It is a very small amount of time out of a whole week. Marriage just isn't one big orgy or one big honeymoon. Even those swingers who are involved in real orgies get bored.

Sex in marriage has become overemphasized in recent years. Don't misunderstand my point. As a friend of mine once said, "Nothing is so short in duration, made up for so quickly, and yet missed so much when it is missing."

The novelty of sex is confined to initial contacts. Once a couple has had sex in all of the different ways they know, and have tried all the methods the sex books describe, that's all there is. Sorry, but unless we run into someone very creative, that's all there will be. After that, everything is just a repeat performance. If you have been to one of the many hard-core pornographic movies, you know that after the first twenty minutes the whole thing becomes boring to watch. One producer of such movies, when interviewed on TV, said he would never go to his own movies because they bored him to tears. It's the same thing over and over. People find that skin-flicks can get dull very quickly. Sex is certainly fun and natural, but two people must work at a depth relationship to insure a lasting marriage that can evolve into real love–the kind that endures because you want it to endure more than anything else.

In terms of having sex, there are certain things people can do that would be helpful in any marriage. During your first sexual experiences you usually were silent. Many couples thus continue to conduct their lovemaking in silence and never change. Sex is more enjoyable when you let your partner know what feels good and what you would like to have him or her do. As most couples mature, they talk to each other more while making love. Knowing how to talk and what to say is important.

A very important consideration in the area of sex is what happens when one says "No" to the other's advances or desires. If you just say "No" to your partner's advances, or "No" to what he or she is doing, you have cut off communication. What does the "No" really mean? If you say, "Don't do that," or "Don't touch me there," you are not giving your partner an alternative. It is much better to say, "Touch me here," or "That feels good," or "Do that some more." In that way you know what your partner would like you to do at that moment, and what feels best. Lovemaking is at its best and most beautiful when it is seen not as receiving pleasure but as giving pleasure. Surprisingly enough, the pleasure that is received by "givers" always seems to exceed that experienced by "takers."

Sometimes the simple act of telling your partner what he or she can do during the sex act gives him or her a sense of greater sexual or physical satisfaction. The process of communicating can heighten the sexual play and increase the sexual pleasure for both the husband and the wife. Remember to avoid "No."

What happens when one partner is not in the mood and the other is? Zap! The turndown! The denial of any bodily pleasures because one partner is not in the mood often leads to misunderstanding. Never simply say "No" when your partner wants to have some sexual fun. Saying "No" again closes alternatives. It would be better to say something like, "How about tomorrow morning?" This leaves some hope and alternatives open in the minds of both partners.

It is up to the one who asked for the delay to live up to the promise when the time comes. All of this should be treated with great care and consideration by each partner. Another put-off or another delay would tend to put stress and strain on the relationship. The promise of sex at another time allows each person to be more prepared for the experience. It is a "mental set" to which you condition yourself–and hopefully with delight. Man's nature is such that unless he is sick or exhausted, he is ready for sex almost any time and without much mental preparation or mood setting. A woman is inclined to be more romantic about it. She takes longer to get into the mood for sex. Many women are offended by men who do not set the stage for such intimate relationships, or who are concerned only about physical satisfaction. Most women become hurt when they feel they are "being used." A husband will do well to be considerate of these psychological differences.

Husbands should realize that women need caresses at times other than when a man wants to go "all the way." It is not uncommon to hear a woman say of her husband that the only time he is romantic is when he wants sex. To show affection just by touching the woman, or holding her close and telling her that she is loved, makes a warmer relationship between husband and wife.

Sex is dependent upon two variables: First, the person with whom a person is having sex is most important in that person's mind; and second, the mood or emotional state the person is in, or wants to be in, while having sex. Foreplay is an important part of the experience. Most of the time a man's nature is such that he seeks little or no encouragement to be in the mood for sex. So red hot may meet ice cold. Couples sometimes don't understand how to cope with these differences and it is important that they learn.

Women have the illusion that men are experts at sex. Men seem to have an image which they think they must live up to. The human male develops sexual awareness much earlier than a female does. Boys start feeling sexual activity around the age of thirteen or fourteen, while in girls this occurs much later. Young girls, sensing the sexual awareness in most young boys, begin assuming that the boys have more knowledge about sexual matters. Adult women should not assume any such knowledge or expertise about men. The husband should not be made to feel inadequate in regard to his sexual expertise. Any relationship between two people, in order to be endearing to both of them, should be built upon mutual trust. Innocence is no impediment to happiness. The fun is in the learning.

A great deal of the sexual enjoyment a couple receives depends on the relationship itself. If a couple are happy together, they can easily work out their sexual problems with a minimum amount of strain. Too many books have stressed sex as the end-all in a marriage relationship. This often has only caused more strain on couples already having sexual problems.

Another key factor to a better sex life is in learning about distraction. Most men do not realize how easily a woman is distracted during sex play. Women are more easily distracted than men. They are apt to think about such things as the children, music, some sudden sounds in the house, or maybe just other things that enter their minds. A nondistracting time, mutually convenient, should be sought for a better atmosphere more conducive to sexual pleasure. The socially busy couple should take the phone off the hook. There are lots of other suggestions that are just common sense. Run away for a weekend and immerse yourselves in sex. A husband should be conscious of trying to develop the sexual desire within his wife, and she should try not to demand more than he can deliver.

Pressure on a man to constantly perform like some sort of superstar can result in a form of impotence. Don't place emphasis on a great performance every time. Our peak experiences are necessarily limited. The more sex is stressed, the more difficult it becomes to perform in the sex act, especially for the male. Relax, be less rigid in your routine, and allow for some spontaneity.

One technique you can use to relieve pressure is to spend an evening together without going "all the way" sexually. Just touch, feel and enjoy each other without expecting the other to perform totally. It feels good and is enjoyable to both. The idea that you are not expected to perform usually relieves the pressure and allows you both to relax. During this relaxation, you will probably develop sexual desire and the physical ability to have sex. Sexual intercourse cannot be achieved merely by willpower. Although many wish it were the opposite, the mind and body must be relaxed. This is probably nature's way of keeping us sane.

Some couples find that eventually their sex life becomes boring. Sex is a routine at bedtime, like taking out the dog or brushing their teeth. They established predictable patterns: the same position, the same motions, or the same sequence of events always at the same time and the same spot. They have fallen into a rut. Most of us run into this problem. Learning how to brighten a dull sex life can be fun and exciting.

One couple I counseled *always* had sex on Saturday morning. It was like a ritual. At my suggestion, a variety of possible times during the day were discussed. This introduced a variety of approaches, times, and places for the couple to creatively enjoy sex. With only a little effort, new life came to the old routine.

If the sex act is a quick routine for you, with a one-two-three and a finish, with no allowance for sustained feeling and caring, you are missing out on a great deal of physical pleasure. You should look for variety in sex. Everything in life, no matter how good or exciting, can get boring and become routine. A change of pace, like having sex at a different time, in a different place, in a different manner–all these help to add to the pleasure and spontaneity.

A universal disappointment that follows shortly after every wedding is that sex is not always Ecstasy Supreme. We fantasize that every time we have intercourse all kinds of new sensual plateaus will be reached–bells will ring and we will be delivered forthwith to a state of heavenly bliss. Time soon enough reveals the difference between the real and the ideal. There are obviously varying degrees of intensity in human feelings. Each of us should realize that neither partner can have the ultimate high in pleasure, physically or mentally, every time we frolic.

Some people compare sex desires to tastes for food. Tastes and appetites vary with each person depending on the time, place, mood, how much and how often. We easily accept these differences. Some people like food exotic and spicy, while others prefer it plain and simple. Most of us agree that too much of the same old unvaried thing becomes tiresome. If you had pork and beans for dinner every night, you would soon grow tired of them. Your inclination will not be to stop eating but rather to change the menu. Although all analogies limp a little, a bit of variety is stimulating where sex is concerned. The time, the place, the approaches, the backdrops–all this can vary and add zest to your sex life. Bust out, loosen up, and be the daring sex idol you fantasized as you looked in the mirror when you were eighteen. You can't do it any better or have any more fun than you can with your spouse.

Go to a show, then out for dinner or dancing like you did when you were dating. Whisper "obscenities" in your partner's ear about how sexy he or she is. Sometimes going to a nearby motel for the weekend and getting away from it all adds the change of pace we all need so much in our fast-paced society.

Having sex in different places is fun. Places like the shower, the couch, the floor–you name it–can make sex more of an adventure. Some of your ideas may be poor. So what. One couple said the place that gave them the greatest thrill was under the pool table in the family room. They hadn't planned it that way, but it just kind of happened one night. (You see, we are all a little nuts at heart.) But it was fun for them. It brought them closer. The essential genuine love and playfulness were there.

There is an abundance of books on the market today that describe different positions for sex. In fact, you can learn a lot more than you want to know. Remember that whatever you want to do in your sex life, providing it is not repulsive to your partner, is fine and you should not be locked in by inhibitions.

While variety in approach is OK, variety in partners can bring trouble. The so-called swinging relationships found in some localities today are not the lasting relationships upon which a couple can build a future. They can be a dead end to marriage. They certainly are a sign of boredom. A person (or a couple) having swinging affairs is trying to get some zing back into his or her sex life. He or she is looking for a rerun on the "freshness" of romance. Some people spend their lives in a constant retreat to youth as if they want to spend their whole lives beginning things that will have no continuation. Who knows why? Perhaps it is just immaturity. Swinging relationships, swap clubs, or whatever, all end in the same way—the men and women involved do not stay together. Swinging marriages seldom go beyond eighteen months. They either break off by mutual agreement or the couple, for a number of reasons, gets a divorce. It is hard for me to understand how genuine love relationships play any part in swinging marriages. It is like saying a person is a trustworthy phony.

The basic idea inherent in all marriages is that the couple have a lasting commitment to each other. The commitment between one man and one woman is lacking in way-out relationships and largely sexually-based attraction. The bachelor pad ultimately fails because most of us want enduring relationships where we can find acceptance, happiness, and a lasting commitment to another. Only icy people can isolate sex, and play it as you would a game. This looks like fun, just like all the "shoot-em-up" movies, but in real life it does not work. Most of us go for warmth, truth, loyalty, and enduring relationships. Civilizations, societies, and marriages have all been built upon commitments and responsibilities that people have to each other. The stability of marriage and good family life is fundamental to any society that will not corrupt itself.

No matter how many times a person is in love, gets divorced and remarries, that person's goal remains the same: He or she is looking for a partner with whom to share life and find acceptance, discover self-worth, and enjoy a happy life.

Somewhere in the evolution of man, sex became tied in with the natural consequence that goes along with having sex. Pleasure is also a part of sex. Sex and pleasure became synonymous with involvement with a person. We have arrived at "no-fault," "no-involvement" sex today because of the new birth control devices. We are now able to approach life with a "thrill-a-minute" mentality. Man has evolved as a being in whom sex gives an illusion of total involvement. Those who would isolate sex from commitment are cornering themselves into a trap. All life becomes an act and only a "gifted phoniness" is real. "I love you" means "I want your body for a little while."

Along with sex and involvement evolved the necessity of intelligent cooperation and thoughtful interaction with another person. Over the years, this process of thoughtful interaction and intelligent cooperation has often been referred to as the common interests that the couple share or the love they have built between them. Love also implies that each partner must allow the other freedom of choice. That is where thoughtful interaction comes into play. Each partner in a marital relationship has freely chosen to be in love with the other. The thrill of being in love is that someone cared enough about you to choose you above all others.

After you fall in love you begin searching, finding, and recognizing the uniqueness in your loved one—above all others. Uniqueness, in this sense, is the high esteem and worth you see in the person with whom you are in love. Love has never yet been adequately defined. Someone has said, "Love is the only strength that makes things one without destroying them." Another perceptive insight reveals that, through love, one creates his own personality and helps others create theirs. Love is indeed life's greatest mystery and its greatest promise.

I can cite example after example of the manifestations of love but, to know what love is all about, you must experience it. Love is a process, and only by experiencing the process can you understand it. To be told about love is like telling a child who has never tasted candy about fudge. A taste can do what words cannot. Once you have had an authentic human relationship, you'll know it is like no other experience you have ever had in your life.

To make a love relationship viable, each of you must see the other as something unique, something special. If you do not see this inner worth, no matter what common interests or other things you have going for your marriage, it is doubtful that your relationship can endure.

What helps to establish lasting relationships are the activities you do and share together. I repeat and emphasize that purely sexual relationships are inadequate. You might try some book or movie suggestions in regard to technique, but it is only your relationship that makes sex more enjoyable. If you care about each other, you will have an enjoyable sexual relationship. This should evolve naturally, unless one or both of you has a problem in this regard. Even so, such problems are easily overcome in a good marriage.

Quite often when a married person has an affair, we think that person has a bad marriage or something is wrong with his or her sex life. Some men and women with good marriages have affairs; some with bad marriages have affairs; and some with in-between marriages have affairs. What usually causes an affair is the "speed" aspect of the relationship. The idea of "speed" as it is used here is discussed in detail in the next chapter. For now let's say it is a chance to get a "zing" or a "thrill." It is a little trip back to the giddiness of youthful romance. Getting to know someone, especially sexually, in a short time (as is done in most affairs) is tingling to anyone's nervous system. It has an air of daring and adventure. Because of the tremendous rate of "speed" that occurs as the two people come toward each other physically and sexually, this sense of thrill is greatly accelerated and becomes overwhelming. And being "forbidden" heightens the adventure.

But when you come right down to making value judgments about your life, sex is not an end in itself but an expression of the relationship that two people who are in love have with each other. And this adventure, like every adventure, can end in tragedy for someone or everyone involved.

In analyzing the differences between love and sex, perhaps this chart will be of help.

LOVE	SEX
Is process. You must go through it to understand what it is.	Is static. You know what it is like somewhat prior to going through it.
Is learned operation. You must learn what to do through first having been loved and cared for by someone.	Is known naturally. You know instinctively what to do.
Requires constant attention.	Takes no effort.
Experiences slow growth—takes time to develop and evolve.	Is very fast—needs no time to develop.
Is deepened by creative thinking.	Is controlled mostly by feeling, that is, responding to stimulus.
Is many small behavior changes that bring about good feelings.	Is one big feeling brought about by one big behavior.
Is an act of will with or without good feelings—sometimes "don't feel like it."	Is act of will. You feel like it.
Involves respect of the person to develop.	Does not require the respect of the person.
Is lots of warm laughter.	Is little or no laughter.
Requires knowing how to thoughtfully interact—to talk—to develop interesting conversations.	Requires little or no talking.
Develops in depth to sustain the relationship—involves much effort—where eventually real happiness is to be found.	Promises permanent relationship but never happens—can't sustain relationship—forever feature is an illusion.

There are several further remarks that should be made. The first is about the misconception that women enjoy or like sex less than men. In the 1970s this generally is not true. Women, as stated earlier, associate sex closely with a person. This does not mean they enjoy sex less than a man. They may view it differently. There are exceptions, of course. I just believe that most women do look for some sort of honest commitment from a man. They don't want to be "used." Throughout history, women have been exposed to "sexual bargains" and all sorts of "sexual offers" from men who want sex without any commitment or involvement. Some women in their search for sexual expression and fulfillment were forced to choose between two basic options: either find sex in marriage or find sex in some socially less acceptable, guilt-associated manner.

Today's world has seen a cultural change. Traditionally repressive environments that rigidly enforced sexual codes upon women (more so than upon men) are rapidly disappearing. The thinking is that women should have the same opportunities as men. But equality is still a hard-fought battle in some corners of American society. The double standard, especially when it comes to sex, fades very slowly.

Most people would agree there has been a general increase in the freedom and responsibility shared by American women since the end of World War II. Also associated with this freedom has come an accompanying sexual liberation for women. Now many women feel freer to express themselves and to acknowledge the enjoyment of sex. And why not?

It is my opinion, however, that some women have greatly misinterpreted this recent sense of freedom. There are those who believe that the new key to finding a mate is promiscuity. In the face of this, I believe that the most important step a single woman can take when seeking a lasting love relationship is to develop as many ways as possible, through common interests and activities, to become authentically involved with a man. The girl who spends all her time in front of a mirror may be missing the point. To be a whole person concerned about her education, personality, authenticity, and ability to communicate and share is vital for the woman who wishes to become involved with a man. This involvement will take place in a great variety of ways, and he will respond to her with a depth of his own. Both interpret the situation as mutual dependency that beautifully fulfills their needs: thoughtfully, emotionally, physically, sexually, and in every other way. They're in love.

The hectic pace of the 1970s has spilled over into married life today. All of us have some concerns in our married lives. We have turned to many sources for answers. Some would have you believe that the main problem in married life today is a terrible lack of knowledge about sex. These people claim that mom and dad are truly ignorant about sex, despite their years of sexual experience. They propose that it is never too late to get a good understanding about the "facts of life." So we are deluged with information about sex from physicians and books and movies and encounters. The problem is sex. The panacea is sex. Others have recommended scientific studies about sex habits and sex practices. Researchers galore have all added to the modern world's knowledge of human sexual activity. Many young people are taught sex education in school. The unfortunate truth is that all this scientific research and all this dissemination of data are not the key to a happier married life. Knowing parts of the human body or twenty-five different sexual positions has little to do with married happiness.

The recent rage of how-to sex books has not even made a dent in the rising divorce rate. A lot of books have been sold. A lot of promises have been made. But couples don't seem to be getting along any better. We might be doing a lot of new things, and maybe in many different ways, but even that hasn't changed the fact that when we cut through all the promises about sex and who is supposed to do what, when, and for how long, what still remains is the close intimacy that two people want, need, and are searching for. And this searching is not just for help in their sex lives but for a way to build their person-to-person relationship so their lives may be truly shared and their love authentic and enduring. Sex is only one part of that relationship. And the real beauty of sex will be the result or reflection of that relationship, rather than the cause. Real love is a priceless gift. Let's face it, anyone can get sex if he wants it. And he can get it on almost any corner if he wants to wait there long enough.

I do not wish to deny the importance of sex in everyone's life. Sex is central to our survival as a species. If it were not important to the human race, we wouldn't be here. Sex feels good, not only physically but mentally, because of the emotions and feeling involved. And I agree that people should be knowledgeable about sex. Just beware of those who promise what no one can deliver: something for nothing. Unfortunately, there are many today whose lives are empty, filled with boredom and loneliness, and to them sex is thought of as a way to find love. For these people, sex offers an immediate, short-term relief because sex always promises involvement *but never delivers*.

For those who have a stronger sense of their own worth, sex becomes less of a way to *find* love and more of a way to *express* an already existing love relationship. I've had many unmarried clients who have told me that, "Once we started having sex, the relationship seemed to fall apart." Sex for these couples somehow seemed to have overwhelmed the somewhat fragile, developing relationship. I really believe that meeting another person to whom you are attracted and growing close, the excitement of living together and sharing life–not knowing where it will lead–of giving one's self, and of receiving love, all overshadow sexual relationships in the total experience of a lifetime. What people ultimately seek from sex is love and an authentic involvement with another human being who really cares about them. None of this will result from sex alone.

Chapter fifteen

From illusion to reality

There are three basic factors present in the interpersonal relationships that develop between two people. These factors come into play the first time two people meet. Let's call the first aspect "speed." The faster the two people move toward each other, the faster is the "speed" in their relationship. The rate of "speed" at which two people move toward each other will vary. "Speed" is unique with every couple. "Speed" is biological. An example of "speed" is when a boy and girl first meet. It feels good just to talk. Later on a date, he puts his arm around her. On the next date, he kisses her. With each step, the "speed" of the relationship is enhanced and they continue to move toward each other. The "speed" accelerates as two people come together. It feels good. The nervous system tingles.

Involvement weekends are a good example of a high degree of "speed." People move very fast toward one another. The problem is, *it doesn't last*. You can only come so close, and after a while, the thrill is over.

Playboy magazine relies on an endless variety of girls to keep the "speed" going. To have the same girl on the centerfold for six months would probably cost them some readers. Variety is the key. There would be no thrill in looking at the same girl month after month. Once you have seen a girl nude in half a dozen poses, that's all there is.

"Speed" demands a new experience or variety to keep it going. Once a couple has had sex many times, the thrill of moving together has ended. The enjoyment of sex hasn't ended, but the "speed" has. And the problem with marriages today is that most of them are based solely on "speed." And if that's all there is, they aren't going to last.

An indication of the significance of "speed" in a relationship is apparent when we find lovers revisiting the places where they spent their first romantic moments together. They love to relive those first experiences. They are full of fond memories, and there is a real joy in reliving those precious moments. What these starry-eyed people did during those romance-filled moments is not really as important as the simple reality that they did it together. But the reliving or returning to old haunts doesn't bring back the zing—only the memories. The biology of coming together doesn't last.

A good example of this can be seen in a young man, Jeff, who came to see me. Jeff told me his marriage had collapsed and his wife had divorced him. He said that he felt badly about the divorce; but in reflecting on his broken romance, he wasn't quite sure what really went wrong. After his first marriage, Jeff met another young attractive woman. They lived together for about a year. After a while the zing in their relationship seemed to disappear. He just didn't feel the same toward her. Somehow she didn't seem to be as much fun as she used to be, even though they were doing some of the same things they had done early in their relationship. He developed mixed feelings about the whole relationship. After their year together he left her. Jeff was now disgusted and disillusioned with his love life. He had observed that the early part of his relationship with most girls was tremendously thrilling, but said that as time wore on he had become bored with all the girls he had ever known. He was searching for the one girl with whom that heavenly sort of feeling would be sustained instead of fading and dying. He wanted to find the spark or flame that would never go out. He concluded by resolving that he was going to search for this person until he found her! In reality he was trying to keep the "speed" going forever–and that is just impossible. We are just not built that way.

Jeff said these were his conclusions when he started living with still another girl. This time he was very cautious since his other two experiences were futile. His third love affair, with a girl named Sylvia, was at this point still rather exciting to him. She was different. He never knew what to expect. Their relationship was a freewheeling one in which they each enjoyed a great deal of freedom. Even though they were sharing an apartment, they both worked and, after work, they frequently went their own ways. Jeff wasn't sure he liked this arrangement, but he thought it was better to see how long his feelings of attraction to Sylvia lasted. They did many things together–like going to dinner at their favorite restaurants, taking turns selecting weekend trips, and doing all the typical things two people might share. But, alas, life with her began to grow a little dull. All those intense feelings were beginning to dwindle. Jeff felt he knew what was coming. He began to wonder if something was wrong with him.

That's when he came to see me. He had to find out whether or not he was normal. He desperately wanted to find the right girl, and he was asking guidance in how he should relate to her so their relationship could be a lasting one. Because he had no close relatives whom he could discuss this with, he was seeking from me some reassurance about the direction in his life.

Jeff's problem is a typical one. He had no problem during the early magnetism of his romance; but then, lacking the knowledge of how to develop the depth that is needed to sustain an interpersonal relationship, he would get bored and break off the entire association. He didn't understand depth, and he didn't understand commitment. He was mesmerized by the thrill of "speed." To accomplish what he wanted, Jeff had to learn how to get involved with his partner in a more meaningful way. His relationships were shallow.

Involvement between two people must be toward other couples with similar interests as well as toward each other. Depth is not always easily developed. Like anything else worthwhile, it takes time and requires work. To sustain it, such a relationship must be ever-deepening. Depth is brought about through a couple's own creative efforts: the things they do together, the common interests they have, what they both share, and the commonality of experiences. The intimate and complete sharing of one's entire life experiences obviously involves a constant deepening of the relationship. Depth, for example, is developed through the mutual struggle to survive economically. The sharing that is required to find a home, pay the mortgage, raise the children, and provide for retirement is enough in itself to create plenty of depth. And to do this especially well, and also share other interests, provides even more depth. Therein lies the secret: There is no limit to our potential for depth. But the potential for "speed" of and by itself is very limited, as Jeff discovered.

Depth must be creatively developed. Two people must *plan* to sustain the relationship today, one that in the past might have been sustained by the very struggle to provide security, much less to survive. When the "speed" had gone, Jeff looked for what else he could do that would keep him interested, amused, or attracted. His relationships had no depth and were largely selfish and one-sided, rather than thoughtful and outgoing–he was immature. By thoughtfulness I mean simply that a person *thinks* of others . . . his partner . . . his lover. He focuses out rather than in. A happy, thoughtful person thinks about others first. This is what Jeff had to learn if he was going to make it in a male/female relationship that would be lasting and meaningful.

Jeff and I began to work out a plan. Helping Jeff to get started on a new path was not a simple process. He had to begin to realize that any meaningful relationship had to be built around more than just the aspect of "speed" and sex and thrills. Jeff said he was willing to work at building a deep commitment with Sylvia. Sylvia was the third woman he had known intimately. At our next meeting we talked about the types of responsibility that grow out of a mature, adult relationship between a man and a woman. These involve a commitment and an eagerness to please the other, to make him or her happy. With this in mind, Jeff set out determined to make things work this time. He was very attracted to Sylvia and did not want to lose her. We embarked on a "Do Plan" that we agreed was realistic for Jeff.

Jeff thought about the things that he and Sylvia liked to do together. He then established his own priorities in a personal action plan. He considered the different things he might do to please her, not just because he wanted her to be happy. For the first time he began working at a relationship, and he was determined to succeed. After awhile, Sylvia sensed what Jeff was doing and she was equally eager to please him and work for his happiness. This is the key to an understanding of love relationships. If both work at the relationship, they will move closer to each other. It is inevitable. Problems will not tear apart a sound marital relationship that is built upon a couple's enduring mutual respect. In fact, problems will be easier to solve and this will further solidify their relationship. It is not the number of problems in a marriage that counts or even the size of the problems themselves. The strength of a deep relationship will enable a happy couple to handle life's many challenges successfully and in stride. Problems that could destroy a weak relationship often will help solidify a strong relationship founded on depth and caring. For example, a child in trouble in a weak marriage is more likely to increase the family tension; and in a strong marriage, a family rallies around the child, giving him the faith and strength he needs to solve his own problems. This in turn usually strengthens the family.

Jeff and Sylvia found many more common interests as they moved closer toward each other, thus increasing the strength of their own relationship. They were thinking about getting married. Jeff's anxiety about developing a lasting relationship was rapidly diminishing. While the "speed" had diminished, it was replaced with a happiness, comfort and dedication that promised to be more enduring. Jeff transformed the "speed" into commitment, and he built a depth relationship around it.

When sex is involved in a "speed" relationship, the rate of the "speed" is greatly accelerated. For example, a man drinking in a night club sees an attractive girl. He buys her a drink, hoping ultimately he can end the evening in bed with her. Here is an example of "speed." The more attractive this woman is, the more intelligent she is, the more status she has, the greater trophy she will make. All this adds to the "speed" that is involved in such a situation.

Quality in a relationship has to do with the value you ascribe to another person. It remains pretty much the same throughout the life of the relationship, unless a person improves himself by doing something like reaching a high degree of competence in a given field. Ultimately, each of us has our own opinion of the quality we give to another person. If our friend in the nightclub does succeed in sexually "making it" with the woman, he has had the thrill of a very fast "speed" relationship. This could have been heightened by his impression of quality in the woman. This is what Jeff was doing in his relationship with the women in his life. He repeatedly sought out attractive women who were also very talented. The thrill of "speed" as they initially moved toward each other was very exciting. He thought of each woman as a person of quality and this made each affair even more thrilling–temporarily. But there was no concept of depth. Until Jeff began to work at an enduring relationship and total commitment, his future with Sylvia was dead-ended. Perhaps there is something to be said for thrill-seekers. I personally find it curious why so many are in constant need of assistance.

How do "speed," sex, quality, and depth relate to a couple after they are married? During the dating stage, the "speed" aspect between two people can be sustained for a surprisingly long time, even for several years. Once the couple decides to get married, and shortly after they are married, the commitment and depth aspect of their relationship becomes paramount.

Let me give you another example of a couple I counseled before their marriage. For some couples this is a routine practice. Sue and George seemed very much in love, and it was easy to see that they had a lot going for them. However, Sue indicated that they had recently been quarreling. Both felt a little uncomfortable about discussing it. During one of our talks, Sue revealed she was beginning to have some doubt whether George really loved her. The increasing frequency of their small spats made her wonder. She was worried about what life would be like after they were married. George was also concerned, but he felt that things would probably work out.

I asked Sue what some of the positive things were that she had tried to do in her relationship with George. She said she tried to develop confidence but that down deep there were reservations. She needed something more specific to give her the confidence and faith she needed that her forthcoming marriage would be a success. I assured Sue that this lack of confidence is not uncommon since marriage is obviously quite a change from single life. I suggested that she make a list of just two or three behaviors of George's that she thought were good. That, she said, would be easy. I asked her to do this every day for a week. She was not to repeat any items on her lists. This was easy for the first three days. Then Sue had to begin to look more thoughtfully at what George was doing. She had already listed those things that were obvious. As a result of the continuing search, after a week or two she began to feel a little closer to George. George and Sue came to the conclusion that perhaps together they should try to make a list of their positive behaviors. They worked at this for three or four weeks. To their surprise, they began to criticize each other less often, and their arguments became less serious. George looked for what he liked in Sue, and she shared her discovery with him. The process itself was fun for both.

Even though George believed that Sue was at least 95% good, when he was upset he would only look at the other 5%. In thinking about the other 5%, George would naturally feel bad because feelings follow behavior. We all have a strong tendency to emphasize faults and overlook virtues in others, especially when there are problems and difficulties. As a former probation officer I once spent an entire day reading the files of the juveniles on record at the court. I did not find one positive statement about any child. I believe we should look for and build on the successes in life rather than the failures; we do this with ourselves whenever we submit a résumé when we seek a job. It always tells the good things we have done, never the bad things.

That behavior is one of life's greatest secrets and greatest gifts: the ability to look at the brighter side. It would be impossible to build a depth relationship with someone about whom we have negative thoughts. Couples cannot afford to wait until they are married to begin to build depth into their relationship. It is vital to base the relationship on a tested confidence, to be certain there is a potential for depth.

Sue became creative about pursuing this depth. She would occasionally write a note to George and mail it, even though they lived in the same city. It was her way of letting him know that she was thinking about him and that she really cared. And George got the message.

I want to add two comments about "speed," quality, and depth before we change the subject. First, these three aspects are all interrelated. It is difficult to separate, isolate, categorize, or label them. This is because all three aspects are directly proportional to the feeling that develops between two people. It is also due to the lack of objectivity we have about ourselves and how we think we relate to other people.

Second, a relationship between two people of the same sex does not usually become as complicated or as intense as do the relationships between a man and a woman. This is because there is no expectation for the relationship to be culminated in sex. "Speed" in a relationship arises immediately as two people are introduced to each other. As two people view each other to be persons of quality and believe each other to be persons who are worthwhile, the feeling is heightened. The depth relationship between two people of the same sex with common interests is easily understandable and less complicated. When the element of sex is introduced, the idea of "speed" and the process of interpersonal relationships just become accelerated and very complex. It is important here to understand the concepts of "speed," quality, and depth that are so basic to the relationship that exists between a man and a woman as they move toward each other. No matter what kind of a relationship, "speed" and quality are felt as tremendously strong. But ultimately depth is the only thing that brings about a true, authentic relationship and keeps it going.

Chapter sixteen

Children and family living

At one time the purpose of marriage was thought to be exclusively for the begetting and rearing of children. The survival of the species was the main concern. During recent years we have expanded our outlook to include other considerations. Today we include in our goals a desire to share and enjoy our lives with a partner. The significance of the change in thinking has affected the overall concept of marriage. Today people have children not just for survival or for farmhands or for the sake of carrying on the family name or heritage, but because they love each other and see their love perpetuated in their children. They want children with whom they can also share their lives.

As they grow and mature into adults, children are often seen by the parents as friends, or as persons to whom they can be close and with whom they can do things. This may sound unusual at first, but consider the increased lifespan during the past half-century. Parents generally live long after their children have been raised and have left home. Many proud parents find great enjoyment and fulfillment in their children and their children's spouses. Many parents, later in life, still enjoy going places and doing things with their married children. Doing things together–such as the entire family spending part of the summer at a cottage, going on picnics, or traveling and vacationing together–is a growing part of American life.

Another important consideration related to children is the recent concern about overpopulation. Planned parenthood is becoming more a part of family living. Very few of us see children as a guarantee that we will have someone to care for us in our old age. The welfare state, along with increased affluence, have made it possible for husband and wife to view children in a different manner.

With apologies to prospective mothers, I will maintain that it is easy to have children. The difficult part is bringing them up.

Depth, as you recall, includes the many things people have in common and the things they do together. Children certainly add depth to the relationship of a husband and wife. The many things each partner must do to bring up children give them a whole world of activity in common. If you're doing your job, there is certainly a lot to talk about. With children there is rarely a dull moment. The house is filled with activity. The children bring home their friends, and the activity quickens. As the children grow older, the variety of things the parents and children can and should do add more and more depth to the total family relationship.

After the children leave, there is somewhat of a letdown and the house can become a lonely place. Because of this change, parents are easily lost. The quiet–it's so very quiet.

Some couples will grow even closer with the children gone and with more time for each other. Some parents develop relationships with their married children that resemble double-dating roles. All of this serves to emphasize the fact that the roles of children and parents have certainly changed in the past several decades.

There is a considerable adjustment necessary for parents who have accepted all the responsibility for their children, to find that they now have no responsibility and no control. For some parents this is little or no problem, while for others the relinquishing of control is difficult to accept.

Parents, heretofore, would judge themselves successful if their children were obedient. It was very common to hear mothers relate how good their children were because, "They always do what I tell them and they never talk back."

Regardless of the child's age, many parents considered this faithful obedience as the center of their obligation and the criterion of their success. As the child grew older and the more he would listen to his parent, the more successful the parent was thought to have been. Many parents hoped to create carbon copies of themselves.

This stifling atmosphere produced many mature "dwarfs." Grown men and women often felt a complete dependency on their parents, and they would be very uncomfortable when making their own decisions. The young married children continued this respect for their parents and were encouraged to continue their reliance for proper decisions on their parents.

Much of this life style has changed. Those who think traditional authoritarianism is very good do not like the seemingly permissive atmosphere of many parent/children relationships today. They hold their children's freedom in considerable check. Children should make their own decisions, regardless of what parents say, because that is the best way to learn responsibility and independence. In either case, today's standards have changed. Most parents consider themselves successful if their children have grown up to be responsible adults. This means the parents have the ability to form authentic relationships with other people and to do things that are worthwhile in the eyes of the child and themselves. Such parents also attempt to implant in their children a conduct respectful of the rights of others.

Years ago if a child grew up and was guilty of some heinous crime, his parents might say that he was a good boy at heart. They might even say, "He would always listen to me. He always respected his parents." Others would seldom fault the parents in such a case. There seemed to be an admiration for parents whose children listened and did a good job.

Today we say that we want our children to be responsible adults, relate to and get along with others, have friends, do things that are worthwhile, and not infringe upon the rights of others. We want them to be independent and responsible for their behavior.

If you ask parents today what they want their children to be when they grow up, you will often hear, "I want them to find fulfillment," or "I want them to do things that are worthwhile, responsible, respectable—and *I want them to be happy*." Not many years ago parents were not too concerned about such issues. There were other overriding concerns, such as eking a living from the land, which were deemed fundamental and primary. Happiness could come later. Survival and security were foremost in the eyes of the pioneers and early generations of Americans who clung to life so tenaciously. That was so not long ago.

Today the notion of responsibility has changed. Responsibility used to be interpreted as doing what those in authority thought you should do. Today the maturing child who is capable of good human relationships, who is able to do worthwhile things and who does not infringe upon the rights of others is considered to be responsible. Parents now teach their children to think for themselves while respecting others. As a child today begins to grow and mature, parents will help their child to understand what he is doing. He will be taught to act responsibly by evaluating what choices he has and by making choices which will achieve his goals without harming others.

Drugs, which include alcohol, are an important problem in our society. Drugs offer a certain kind of involvement. Children who have friends and feel confident about themselves and who know their parents care about them are seldom involved with drugs. They have many rewarding involvements. They don't need the illusory happiness offered by drugs.

Drugs, especially alcohol, are readily available, but they have little to offer the child who is eager about life and his friendships and the worth of what he does. The companionship of friends and parents is sufficient so that drugs are not necessary to stem a feeling of loneliness. The reason children take drugs is to rid themselves of the pain of loneliness. Never forget, we *learn* how to love; it doesn't come naturally. We learn this through those who care about us, through example—especially that of our parents. If a child grows up with nothing but fighting and hate, that's all he learns. Yet we have a built-in need to be with people, a need to make friends, a need to love. Like any need in our human system, if it goes unfulfilled, we will eventually feel pain. Loneliness is our nervous system telling us we need to make friends. If a child hasn't learned how to love, and is rejected in his attempts to make genuine friendships, he is going to feel the pain of loneliness. He has no choice. The pain comes automatically if we experience rejection. Unfortunately, most adults don't understand this. If I had a gaping hole in my tooth and the nerve was showing, I surely wouldn't want the tooth drilled without Novocain. Yet I wouldn't be considered a drug addict. Most everyone understands the pain of a toothache. Yet, because most of us haven't experienced the real pain of loneliness we don't understand it. Thus, we have little sympathy for the child who drowns himself in alcohol or loses himself on hard narcotics to get rid of the horrible pain of loneliness, emptiness and boredom which fills his life. Psychological pain is far worse than physical pain, yet few have much sympathy and little understanding for these children. Only the love and concern of another can in any way help these children.

Thus parents should be involved with their children, especially when they are young. This should take the form of support, encouragement and involvement rather than domination. This parent/child involvement, like a marriage, must be constantly worked at and maintained for it to grow and mature.

Some recent studies claim that parents spend, on the average, only seven and one-half minutes a week in thoughtful interaction with their children. The effect of such isolation is usually an indescribable loneliness. The parents who do nothing but watch TV with their children and then feel that they have spent an enjoyable evening with the family are only kidding themselves. There is no social interaction involved. The children are not learning anything from or about their parents. The parents are not relating to their children. Each might as well be in his own room.

Many "video orphans" grow up without any real affection for their parents. And the parents wonder why. Many children today lack the closeness of relationships that families of earlier generations had. Today when closeness is more vital than it ever was, many children experience complete personal isolation. They have parents who will share a house and food and clothes, but who will not share the most important thing in the world to their child–they will not share themselves.

Some examples of thoughtful interaction in families can be derived from the games that families can play together. Scrabble, Monopoly, and Tripoley are good games that bring the family closer together. As the children grow, bridge and chess are fun and instructive. Talking thoughtfully about interesting things is fun. Dinner table discussion is very important. Other things that build interaction and bring families closer together are such household projects as painting and working in the yard; also action games are fun, such as pool, Ping-Pong, basketball, touch football, badminton, and lawn darts. The sharing of fun stimulates conversation. The family members talk to each other and laugh and enjoy each other's company. This involvement brings with it a psychological presence, as well as a physical, mental and social presence. This is what the child remembers. This is what draws him to the family.

Parents should realize it is necessary for children to feel that there is a part of the house where their friends will be welcome. Whether it be a bedroom, family room, den, living room, kitchen, or some other room, it is important that children feel accepted with their friends in their own home. Also important to a child's sense of belonging is that he is able to bring a friend home for dinner. The talk and social interaction among the family members around the table make the children feel wanted. Children develop a deeper sense of importance and feel they are an integral part of the family. Such children tend to develop stronger and more secure identities.

There is certainly nothing wrong with making some parts of the house off-limits for certain children's activities. Discipline and respect are as important as freedom, and indeed they lead to real freedom. In balance, children should be made to feel comfortable in their home.

Children should be encouraged to play with other children. On his own, among others, a child learns the give-and-take necessary to get along in life. His creativeness is encouraged when he is playing with peers. Expensive toys are not essential. Blocks, crayons, paper, simple games and materials that lend themselves to creativity are more than sufficient. The intensive involvement most children seek in playing with friends develops emotional stability. Children learn to enjoy others, to settle their differences and to play creatively and happily.

As I mentioned earlier, television watching should be limited. Discuss the programs with your child. Be selective and control the amount of TV. Parents who allow their children to watch television endlessly have created a new problem: When there isn't a TV program that intrigues the child, the reaction is, "I'm bored; I don't have anything to do." TV may be a fine diversion, but it is a poor substitute for involvement. Before TV, children were more creative and resourceful with their playtime.

No matter what a parent suggests to the child who can't find a TV program to watch, there is a long face. What can a parent possibly suggest that is more amusing than TV? Even though the parents go through a whole host of suggestions, our television "addict" will have none of it. He'd rather watch a test pattern. Parents might proceed to tell the children how they played with boxes or pots or went outside to play tag or hide-and-seek when they were kids. I have found the best way to get a child to do something is to do it with him. Children learn by doing things with others.

The gap today between parent and child is not as much a generation gap as it is a cultural gap. Children today are geared to a much quicker tempo. "Sesame Street" teaches them to count in rapid succession. It is fun and amusing because of its pace. When the child is taught by a parent or teacher who slowly says "One . . . two . . . three . . ." or "A . . . B . . . C . . . ," the child, being oriented to a much faster pace, becomes bored. Also the child has been conditioned by TV to be both passive and still be amused. He can be kept busy and not emotionally threatened. The TV set doesn't ask questions that might be embarrassing. Even if the TV poses embarrassing questions, the child can simply ignore them.

Parents spend too much time analyzing why their child has done something. This is often a waste of time. Once you know why, all you know is why. This in itself doesn't solve anything. Parents should get the child to evaluate what he is doing and help him make a plan for what he is going to do in the future. In dealing with anyone, it is better to stay away from past faults and deal with present behavior. Typical phrases that kill effective communication are, "Oh, you've done that again. I told you last week that if you ever did that again I was going to tell your father," or "Don't you ever learn? You promised me you weren't going to do that," or "How could you do that to me?" The parent goes on and on and is really not solving anything by belaboring the point without offering any constructive alternatives.

Success experience is vital for every child. Success behaviors are very important. Allowing children to continue in failure situations is very detrimental to a child's potential. The only thing a child learns from failure is how to fail. The reinforcement provided by success, no matter how small, is vitally important to a child's development of worth and identity. The over-zealous parent who forces a child to try something in which the child has little chance to succeed is being most unfair to the child. Every child will experience some failures, and he easily learns to cope with occasional setbacks. It is the important duty of a parent, whatever the cost and at whatever level the child must be placed, to see that success experience and confidence are developed. Some parents have many excuses like, "Oh, it will be good for him to go through that. It will build character." Or, "After you try it, you'll like it." Or, "Do it for dad . . . or mom . . . or grandma. . . ." Children should never be encouraged to try things when they don't have a chance to succeed.

You must plan so that your children will be given experiences and afforded opportunities wherein they find success and growth. It is upon such success experience and the confidence it creates that people build their lives. The rule is really simple: Pleasure feels better than pain and success feels better than failure. Those things which give us pleasure we continue to do. Those things which give us pain we avoid or at least try to avoid.

Involvement with your children is really the greatest gift you, as parents, can give. Money and material things can spoil and destroy your children. The things they will remember about you as their parents are the things you enjoyed together. They will remember how you shared yourself with them. Children remember all the moments and happiness you constructed by your sharing. The value system of youngsters revolves around their involvements with those they love. They will forget the expensive toys and the fancy clothes, but they themselves will live out the love they experienced. This is how morality is taught; we teach our children what we believe by the way we live, not by what we say. The greatest gift any parents can give their children is love plus an unselfish sharing of themselves. And this is found in time, for nothing will take the place of time spent with children. This is the key to a happy home.

Chapter seventeen

How open a marriage?

Bill is a mechanic for an automobile dealer and is very happy with his job. He and his wife, Sally, and their two preschool children live in a middle-income neighborhood. Sally keeps house, takes care of her children, and has no intention of going to work.

Bill makes enough money to keep his family in necessities, with a little over for recreational activities. Sally rarely complains when Bill goes out with the boys for bowling or golf. She has her own club, which she attends once every two weeks.

Bill makes most of the decisions and Sally is satisfied with this arrangement as long as the bills are paid and he takes her out occasionally. She would love to have more affection and attention, but she sees this as an ideal to be hoped for, rather than a reality to be achieved.

The commitment between husband and wife will vary. Each couple works out a pattern that is comfortable for them. The marriage of Bill and Sally may be the type that is well suited to a large number of people. On the other hand, it may be that the older, traditional marriage is what many today find very uncomfortable. In this instance, one mate dominates and sees marriage as a way to live, rather than as a developing love relationship. Today many couples realize they must work out a marriage that is consistent with their life style and then develop their pattern accordingly. Still other marriages have very little commitment between the partners. These are marriages nevertheless, and somehow the arrangement survives. The couples seem to enjoy this type of limited commitment to each other. They believe this kind of relationship permits them more freedom and opportunity for growth. And there are still those who look for total commitment to each other. They believe that their happiness lies in the effort they put forth in working at their marriage and living in very close union.

However, the marriage with a limited commitment seems to be much more innovative in our present culture. This new marriage is clearly defined because it is so new. There is no strict interpretation of the new marriage; but there is limited commitment between partners, and they will define their marriage as an honest and open relationship based on the concept of equal freedom and identity. Each partner has an equal right to grow as an individual within the marriage. The new marriage is supposedly based on a verbal, intellectual, and emotional commitment–to the effect that each partner is free to move and create his own future. Few of us would take issue with the principles that man and woman should be equal partners in marriage, and that each person should have the right to individual growth and maturity.

A problem arises when we consider how free each person should be to move in the world. Proponents of this marriage obviously feel it to be a considerable liability and a dehumanizing limitation not to be "free to move." There is an underlying premise of the new marriage that seems to imply that these two people are not necessarily going to remain sexually faithful to each other.

This concept of marriage is somewhat new in the history of man's social evolvement. It is definitely something new in Western civilization, which is the foundation of our culture. People who embark on such a marriage, with its limited commitment and openness to sexual infidelity, should understand that they are involved in something new and untested. Their commitment in marriage is subjected to periodic and annual, if not constant, review. All this is new as a structural approach to marriage.

Our major concerns have altered. We have, so to speak, taken on other worries. Now we look to marriage no longer as an economic security blanket but something which hopefully will relieve the loneliness, the boredom, and the emptiness that seem to have engulfed our people.

We are looking for something in the relationship, something to fill our lives with happiness and a contented ease. The failure to find this happiness is reflected in the recent increase in the singles syndrome, whereby thousands of unattached men and women find this life an end in itself–somewhat reflecting the failure of the institution of marriage.

But even those couples who have been married for some time are now trying to adjust to this new way of life. Some have shifted their attention from just going to a job to an awareness of how to make the marriage work. Others are preoccupied with amusing themselves while exerting less effort at making their marriage work. Television fills most of the leisure hours for many, while others are taking a new look at their lives, and especially their marriage, in hope of finding a more rewarding relationship.

Even in a new marriage two people will tolerate sexual infidelity only because they hope it will make the marriage stronger. The object is to make their lives happier and not more miserable. Those who prefer this "new marriage" will find it will probably strengthen the relationship in a few cases, but it won't strengthen it for the vast majority. Unless two people can handle this kind of relationship, it will be a miserable fiasco. Seldom will a couple arrive at this kind of arrangement by mutual consent. Most of the time one will go along with it because he or she feels it is what the other wants. Thus one partner is sort of pressured into the relationship. The person being pressured hopes that by going along the new open marriage will improve. The partner who wants the change evidently feels some kind of change is needed to allow for personal growth.

Open marriage, as I see it, is a relationship of peers or equals in which there is no need for one person to dominate the other. Proponents say that traditional marriages are relationships requiring one person to be submissive to the other. Usually advocates of new marriage single out the male as being the villainous figure who led a life of a double standard and required his wife to be something of a faithful homebody. This is gross distortion, as many happily married couples will tell you. The idea that men always dominate households is ridiculous and simply not true. In many cultures the woman rules the roost. In our culture one will frequently find the woman to be the dominant personality. The father in many situations is simply the breadwinner, while ma calls the shots. One cannot make generalizations about male or female personalities in such a way as to predict who might dominate a marriage.

Also, it has been stated by some who believe in the new marriage that man is not by nature monogamous. I believe he is. A review of the many cultures and sociological conditions in man's human evolvement seems to indicate that man is by and large a social being who does make and has made lasting commitments with a mate for life.

To shed further understanding on the changing relationships, we should look at what is going on today. There is little doubt in my mind that relationships of all types are becoming more tenuous and less stable. We move from city to city and from state to state and from one end of the country to the other. Whenever a culture takes on such rapid mobility, the characteristics of strong, permanent relationships just become harder for people to establish and maintain. When we were an agricultural nation and people stayed on the family farms, folks seldom left the county or city in which they were born. Relationships were much more permanent, lasting, and enduring. Establishing new relationships was not something we worried about several generations ago, but it worries a lot of people today. We live in large cities and worry about not having any really close friends. Most of us are lonelier than ever, and we find it far more difficult to find and to keep good friends. We meet and pass thousands of people, often the same people every day. We pass as strangers.

The anonymity of apartment living can result in extreme loneliness and misery. Even people living in traditional single-family dwellings say they often don't even know their neighbors. Social groups which have been a strong part of man's heritage since civilization began have been recently placed under great stress. Social workers and psychologists, confronted by the many symptoms of a rapidly changing, mobile society, have made various suggestions intended to help people confront their problems. A few of the less conventional people will experiment with group marriages, swapping partners for an evening, a month, or a weekend. Communes are not new. They have existed in varying sizes and structures throughout history. Few communes have encouraged free sex. Serial marriages, sometimes called sequential monogamy, have been predicted as a result of so many going through one divorce after another.

Is there an answer? Perhaps in searching we should look at how our society has evolved over the centuries. There is no doubt that to survive as a species man has relied upon his adaptability and his ability to reason. The family unit has been the fundamental, basic ingredient essential to man's preeminence. The social group and the larger organized society are also fundamental to our successful life structure, and to our adaptability to the world around us. Even apes and gorillas have strong family units or clans, and so they have rules and their own limited kind of social organization. Some form of order and structure is essential for the progression of life in an orderly, civilized manner. Marriage is the basic and vital institution fundamental to the hierarchical structure of man's culture.

Marriage is more important today than ever because it is the underpinning of our whole social structure. It is the answer to loneliness, mobility, and fragmentation. Some people argue that marriage is an outdated social institution. They hold that marriage cannot keep pace in this age of technology and science. Instead we should have free marriages based on nonpermanent relationships wherein there is no deep commitment. This is convenient to both parties and involves only limited commitments, which can be easily terminated should either party decide not to work at the relationship. Infidelity is acceptable because human beings are just animals of a higher order, and whoever invented monogamy is as out of date as the corset.

A study of man's cultural past will not sustain arguments for the "new marriage." Even prehistoric man did not live in promiscuous bands of rape-happy men who dragged women off to their caves. Fundamental to prehistoric man's success was the family unit, a closely knit structure that enabled man to survive the elements, as well as to avoid becoming the main course for larger, stronger animals. Man survived not only because of his mental tenacity but because the family and social structure of clans and related groups gave him an organized way to defend the group and provide for their needs. Man outlasted other forms of life because he formed deep commitments to his mate, his family, and his relatives, and he intelligently cooperated with his fellow man. The same is no less true today.

Social structures were necessary to a social being. Besides survival, there are other reasons, all of which enable man to lead an organized, predictable and happy life. For example, when you drive your car and approach an intersection, you expect traffic signals or road signs to control dense traffic and prevent chaos. Primitive man saw the need for an organized life, and he designed institutions and systems that would enable him to improve his situation. Marriage is a very basic example of such an institution. Although marriage in prehistoric times was not as ritualistic as it is today, it was for the most part a one-man/one-woman relationship. The family unit was based on one man and one woman and the children they had together. Even then they had commitments to each other. They worked together, loved each other, braved a tough and sometimes cruel world, and sought a happy existence.

My conclusion is that the new marriage, lacking in depth of commitment (if indeed it varies from promiscuity), is a new and risky experiment coming at a time when we need all the friendship and security we can get. I believe marriage to be a maturity based relationship in which two people make and keep commitments. Marriage will be what you make it. The possibility that "oneness" stifles and hinders creativity and growth must be weighed against the certainty that promiscuity creates chaos. Some cry for identity, a separate identity. However, whenever two people are happily married, their lives become so intertwined that they do not have a totally separate existence. No man really lives his life alone. It is only through others, and especially those we love deeply, that we find ourselves. Although each of us is unique, there is a natural and social dimension that we have very much in common. Although times and customs change, they, in essence, remain very much the same. There are many forms and varying degrees of commitment in marriage based on what each couple finally determines their life together ought to be. In this chart, the vast continuum of marriage styles has been reduced to three distinct types so they can be more easily evaluated.

ONE MATE DOMINATING THE OTHER	TWO INDEPENDENT LIFE STYLES	SHARING OF LIVES
Denial of self	Personal growth	Giving of self, in order to receive
No review	Marriage commitment is subject to review	What you can do to make things better is subject to review
Marriage above all else	Person above all else	Relationship or sharing above all else

DOMINATING	INDEPENDENT	SHARING
Male has rigid role expectations; female has rigid role expectations	Reversal of roles or roles independent of marriage	Doesn't matter who does what
Nothing changes	No roles defined–thus, possibly no movement	Not important who does it, but 1) it gets done, 2) they do it together
sex		
Absolute fidelity (never looking at someone else)	Infidelity sanctioned	May be attracted to someone, but relationship and commitment are enough to make infidelity unnecessary
love		
No growth, static–tied to paternal and maternal responsibility	Growth comes mostly independent of each other	Growth comes from working at relationship
identity, growth		
Subservient to marriage–identified as husband or wife, not as person	Comes from doing your own thing	Comes from 1) the development of the relationship and 2) doing things which you believe to be of value or worth
each other		
Taken for granted	Mixture of love and being taken for granted	Constant development of relationship and growth toward each other
trust		
Not thought of–expected	Not required to any great degree	Seen through what you do
children		
Probably seek carbon copies; focus will be on obedience	Vulnerable to the tenuousness of the relationship; if the parent gets an urge to grow, the kids must go	The product and the object of love and concern–raised to be themselves with respo[illegible]sibility and success as a foundation

What form of marriage you choose is, of course, your choice. Each of us chooses the kind of marriage with which we can feel comfortable. We may be influenced by our peers, our parents, our church, or our community. It is important, however, to be aware of what options there are.

Remember, you can only work at what you personally can do in the marriage; you can't change other people. If you are trying a new type of marriage, you are probably in for some shocks and surprises. There is no doubt that marriage is a contract. There is no doubt that marriage is an institution basic to society, one which enables a man and woman to seek a new and a good life together. But the contract of marriage is more than a legal one. Marriage is also a psychological and emotional union. This union does not mean the husband and wife stop their growth and maturation. The marriage contract does not limit the couple's growth. Instead, it suggests you are mature enough to think so much of your loved one that together you are now willing to share your lives, in good times and in bad, in good health and in bad. A reading of the vows makes it obvious that this is a mature decision. It is a milestone in your life.

The key to understanding a successful marriage is that you are willing to think of the other partner first and you are willing to work at your relationship. Maturation and growth is a goal worth working toward. Like a flower, each unselfish person will open a little at a time. Your happiness is in seeing what you can do for your partner. To the extent that we are able to focus out, we begin to grow. If you cannot move toward your spouse, then toward whom can you move closer? If you want to be outgoing and to mature, what better place to start than through your marriage?

In an open marriage each is supposed to be free to do his own thing. In my opinion this can reduce your involvement in the marriage. This relationship is so structured that there is less dependence on the other. And here I define dependency as our needing another, not for what he or she can do for us but as someone toward whom we can move. *We need to work at loving others for our own sake, not for theirs.* It is we who gain when we love another. For another to gain, he or she in turn has to work at loving us. That is the paradox of love. With less dependency there will obviously be less involvement. *Whenever there is less involvement there is greater danger that the relationship will not be strong enough to endure the stress of everyday living.* Am I safer because I promised less? Am I more mature because my relationship is tentative? Can real love have reservations? Or is love like everything else today—fleeting, fanciful, fragmental, phony? I wonder if this type of marriage will be easily sustained when it is founded on doubt.

Man is evaluative. Look at all the charts, diagrams, and market reports in your daily newspaper. We are constantly evaluating how we are doing and whether what we are doing is making us happy. The fact that we had something to eat, had a roof over our head, had kids that were happy and had money in the bank was once sufficient to make us feel content. Not today. The evaluative process has become refined to a point where acknowledgement of our popularity or acknowledgement of our new coat adds to our feeling of self-worth. We are very sensitive about our image.

The reason for the big increase in loneliness and just plain boredom that fills our land is due, I believe, to our increased awareness and concern over our image and our relationship to others. In marriage, this choice is even more critical.

We behave and live our lives pretty much the way we view ourselves. Our choice of life style in our own marriage will ultimately pay off in our own happiness in life. The choice we make is our own.

Chapter eighteen

Marriage: past, present, future

Marriage: Past

Most people would agree that marriage, like the rest of the world, has been constantly changing. Perhaps personal relationships such as those found in marriage were never intended to be static. In the early days of our country, little thought was actually given to the formal institution of marriage.

Many today believe that frontier life was romantic with its robust men and beautiful women, matinee variety. In real life, if there was one outstanding characteristic of the frontier housewife, it was her smoke-reddened eyes and tight, dry complexion. Beauties were few and far between. Have you ever seen any photographs taken in frontier days? Most of a woman's time was spent cooking at an open-hearth fire. The labors of frontier life, improper diet, disease and exposure resulted in mostly sallow and sickly men. The normally pregnant woman had scads of children to rear. Many women died in the process.

Premarriage romanticism was also idealized in the colonies. This was followed by almost universal post-marriage male dominance. The men were the protectors, the property owners, the voters, the authority. This continued in America until about the time of the woman's suffrage movements. Both world wars did much to change the lot of women, and so came changes in their roles, identities and life patterns. Women discovered they could do most things as well as men and some things better. This realization gave women a new self-concept as human beings of competence and capacity. Mothers, yes, but more than mothers they could be. This marked the beginning of the end of the male-dominated and male-structured society in America. During this same period, contraceptive devices were being perfected, allowing women to enjoy the sex act without fear of an unwanted pregnancy.

It is interesting to note that the American family's major concerns in the 1930s and the 1940s were to have food on the table, a roof over their heads and, perhaps, a few of those things we now call basic creature comforts, like a washing machine. But they were not basic then. They were highly sought after. People could not afford many creature comforts, and anything beyond a simple living and being clothed, fed, and kept warm was usually considered a luxury. Many people still live like that in some parts of America where basic necessities are the only concern. In spite of this, our country has never been so affluent. The minimum standard of living is generally on the rise for almost every American family. Granted, in many parts of our country poverty is still very real and very severe, but among the young in these areas TV has helped to create the illusion that everything is going to be better.

Marriage: Present

Now in the age of the welfare state, where most of us enjoy considerable leisure, men and women are no longer just satisfied to simply survive and keep the family together. The criterion of success in marriage and raising a family has changed from mere cohabitation to a happy and growing interpersonal relationship. The whole idea of pleasure and personal fulfillment is somewhat of a new departure in an American culture that has been based on the Puritan ethic of hard work.

The industrial and business world reduced the work week from fifty-some hours weekly on the average to the low forties. Vacations were extended. There was more and more time for leisure pursuits. And right into this time vacuum came the television set. Television moved us rapidly into significant cultural change. TV offered instant escape and diversion to a people who had just been through a terrible war and whose parents had experienced a disastrous Depression.

Economic growth continued and with a new emphasis on credit buying, many so-called luxuries became available to a large part of the population. Whatever you want, get it now and pay later. And so came a shift from frugality to instant gratification. Why save everything for a tomorrow that may never come? Remember the Depression. Remember the war. Live it up while you can. The more luxuries you have, the happier you will be. There is something new every minute, and more on the way.

All this has led to a significant cultural change. The contrast might be viewed in the manner shown in the following chart.

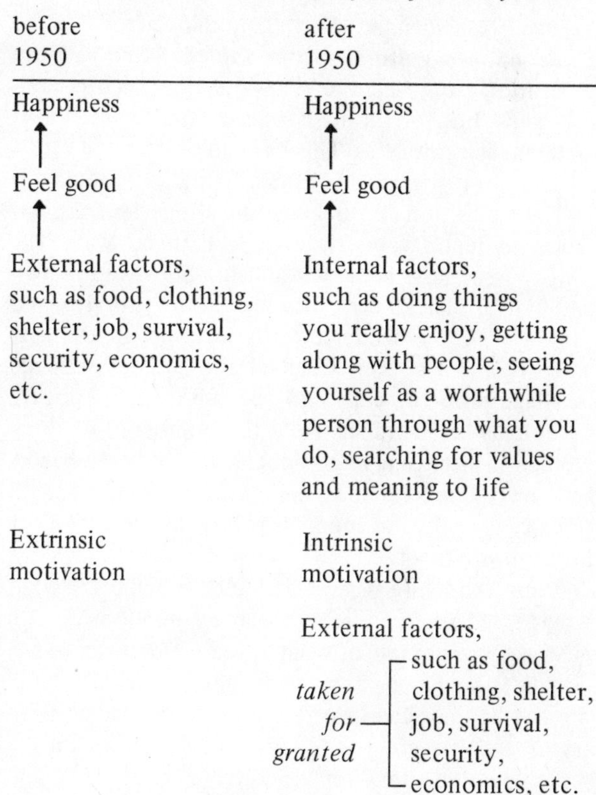

It is very important to realize that it was in the very act of "struggling to make it" in the pre-1950 security society that brought love to the relationship. Today, there is very little economic struggle, and security is taken for granted. The primary motivation is now intrinsic.

Today's younger generation, as a result, is less concerned with issues of survival and economics. Personal happiness and fulfillment take precedence. Happiness is now measured in doing things worthwhile and not exclusively associated with economic factors. So we come upon a cultural gap in values. Some call it a generation gap. And there have always been generation gaps, but for the first time we find a significant difference in priorities. This has had a profound effect on modern marriages and family living.

The transition from economically oriented marriages to identity marriages is well under way. The central issue now is the relationship between the man and woman. They know they are going to survive, and they are not preoccupied with security. In the past when the man became disabled and unemployed, the marriage probably collapsed because he could not fill his role as breadwinner. Now the number of working women is increasing at an unbelievable rate. Marriages seldom collapse for the same reasons. Number one in priority now for the couple is getting along and enjoying their life together.

Many today are having difficulty in achieving what is expected from a modern marital relationship. I'll give you an example of what I mean. Donna and Fred couldn't understand why their marriage wasn't working out as they had hoped. Donna said she had been trying to be a good wife. She had his meals on the table when he came home, kept the house clean, and took care of their three young children. What else did he expect? She was patterning her role in a modern marriage after a survival/security marriage where this kind of performance was all that was expected.

Fred was somehow restless and discontented. He was trying to make things work out. He put in his eight hours at work, came straight home, earned a good paycheck, and was handy around the house. But all of these things weren't making him happy. Fred was operating with a survival/security mentality. The couple was young and "with it." They sensed a certain emptiness. They were aware that something was missing, but at a loss to determine what they were doing wrong. So here were Fred and Donna looking for a way to build a better marriage.

My task was to help them look beyond the issues of sex and financial security. They had arrived at a new frontier in interpersonal relationships; it required a sharing of likes and interests that bring involvement and enjoyment to both people. Donna was first-rate in practical matters, but equally as important was how she was rated as a friend and a companion. Fred, too, had to do more than provide security and bring home a paycheck. Together they faced a challenge to deepen a relationship that might have bordered on an ideal just a generation ago.

This is the cornerstone of modern marriage—the need of both parties for a truly deep, rewarding relationship in which both can find happiness. The male and female stereotyped images are rapidly changing. The man seldom has a standard list of tasks that he is expected to perform. Changing a diaper is no longer strictly a woman's concern. Today we have come to a point where there is no preordained structure to the division of labor. A good arrangement is one that works well. There is more sharing in marital responsibilities. These significant cultural changes are taking place right before our eyes. It is truly remarkable to be living through such a time as this—and to be aware of and a part of this historic development.

Marriage: Future

What will marriages be like in the future? A few foresee serial marriages, or progressive monogamy, where men and women will have a succession of marriages with one partner after another throughout their lifetimes. They predict serial marriages will last from five to ten years and then the couple will break up, each in search of new personal growth. Divorce rates are climbing rapidly and the advent of no-fault divorce could be an indication of this possibility. I personally feel that such transient structures are not consistent with human nature, and not conducive to human growth. There is adequate evidence of this in the lives of the divorced. The concept of serial marriage is more likely an indication that we are not working intelligently enough at sustaining our interpersonal relationships. What many people are trying to achieve is involvement without much effort. Here you have the rapid rise in popularity of the singles' complexes. When the relationship becomes difficult, say good-bye and find another. It is easier to start over. Maybe next time things will work out. If not, try again. But don't get too close or you'll get caught.

Another projection occasionally made about future marriages is a type of communal arrangement. This is by no means a new concept. Even American history records a significant number of such experiments. All, without exception, have failed. Communal marriage is in stark contradiction to our typical images of individuality and love and loyalty. Many of these notions are fascinating in concept but frustrating in application. Communes based on monogamy may be possible, but at this writing there is no compelling reason for such a structure. Our present system of monogamy can and does work. The basic reason for this is that nothing is as personally rewarding as a good relationship between a husband and wife. Every good relationship must be worked at, and no structure can replace this individual responsibility.

The sexual promiscuity in swap clubs and similar endeavors are attempts by some people to find authentic involvement with a person who really cares about them. Bizarre as it may seem, this leap into carnality does attract some people. This also is not new, nor does anyone take seriously the possibility that such dehumanizing activity can lead anywhere.

I believe marriages of the future will continue to be what they are today—one man and one woman in a close personal relationship. There are a great many reasons why this type of relationship will continue. One reason is simply the joy of love two people find together as husband and wife. Another reason is that the marriage/family concept as it is known today is the best way to bring up children. It is also the best way to teach children the meaning of love and concern. Children in a home where real warmth and loving relationships are apparent will want and seek the same warm and loving relationships in their own lives. Basically all children learn about love relationships by observing and imitating others. If all they experience in a home is fighting, children learn little about love; what they do learn is how to fight. To a large extent children are a reflection of the home in which they are raised. If their home is full of laughter and love, the children will live and spread what they have learned.

Marriage as we know it is a relationship that adds stability and continuity to the ongoing process of living. We live in a world of constant change and the pace of change is constantly accelerating. Add to this the idea of constantly changing partners, as some predict, and you may have a very hectic and confusing result. The instability of relationships will only detract from our ability to cope with change. The offices of the nation's counselors are filled now with neurotic victims of our fast society. Security and stability require some kind of constant.

Once you put money in a bank, you don't have to work at keeping it there. It is tangible security. You can depend on it. It won't die off. It is there when you need it. Friendships, such as marriages, do not offer this type of security. You can't establish a relationship and just expect it to stay there. Marriages must be continually worked at. If we would only spend as much time in establishing more depth in our present marital relationships and in preparation for marriage, there would be many happier marriages and many fewer divorces. The willingness to accept the responsibility to work at a relationship is the key to the future and the key to happiness. Throughout the centuries, there has really been no other happiness as blissful and endearing as the relationship that is found when two people who love each other come together. True, authentic married love gives purpose to life and hope for the future. I see nothing else that can or will replace this reality.

Those interested in Reality Therapy
are invited to contact:

William Glasser, M.D.
Institute for Reality Therapy
11633 San Vicente Boulevard
Los Angeles, California 90049

Edward E. Ford, M.S.S.A.
10209 North 56th Street
Scottsdale, Arizona, 85253

Edward E. Ford is an Associate of the Institute For Reality Therapy. He has acted as a consultant and conducted workshops on Reality Therapy for the Ohio Youth Commission, numerous rehabilitation and mental health facilities, school districts, social service organizations and universities. Mr. Ford, a former high school teacher, is a graduate of Case Western Reserve University's School of Applied Social Sciences. Along with writing and lecturing on Reality Therapy, he is in private practice a marriage and youth counselor.

Robert L. Zorn, Ph.D., is presently serving as Assistant Superintendent of the Mahoning County Office of Education in Youngstown, Ohio. He has experience as a teacher and principal on elementary and high school levels, has served as a consultant to many school districts and has published numerous articles in various publications.

8 9 0